THE
INDISPENSABLE
GUIDE
to practically
EVERYTHING

Bible Prophecy
and End Times

THE
INDISPENSABLE
GUIDE
to practically
EVERYTHING

Bible Prophecy
and End Times

DOUGLAS CONNELLY

Guideposts
New York, New York

The Indispensable Guide to Practically Everything: Bible Prophecy and End Times

ISBN 13: 978-0-8249-4772-9

Published by Guideposts
16 East 34th Street
New York, New York 10016
www.Guideposts.com

Distributed by Ideals Publications, a division of Guideposts
2636 Elm Hill Pike, Suite 120
Nashville, Tennessee 37214

Guideposts and *Ideals* are registered trademarks of Guideposts.

Acknowledgments
Every attempt has been made to credit the sources of copyrighted material used in this book. If any such acknowledgment has been inadvertently omitted or miscredited, receipt of such information would be appreciated.

Scripture quotations marked CEV are from the Contemporary English Version, copyright © 1995 by the American Bible Society. Used by permission.

Scripture quotations marked HCSB are from the Holman Christian Standard Bible®, copyright © 1999, 2000, 2002, 2003 by Holman Bible Publishers. Used by permission. Holman Christian Standard Bible®, Holman CSB®, and HCSB® are federally registered trademarks of Holman Bible Publishers.

Scripture quotations marked MSG are from *The Message*. Copyright © 1993, 1994, 1995, 1996, 2000, 2001, 2002. Used by permission of NavPress Publishing Group.

Scripture quotations marked NASB are from the New American Standard Bible®, copyright © 1960, 1962, 1963, 1968, 1971, 1973, 1975, 1977, 1995 by The Lockman Foundation. Used by permission.

Scripture quotations marked NIV are from the Holy Bible, New International Version®. Copyright © 1973, 1978, 1984, International Bible Society. Used by permission of Zondervan Publishing House. All rights reserved.

Scripture quotations marked NKJV are taken from the New King James Version. Copyright © 1982 by Thomas Nelson, Inc. Used by permission. All rights reserved.

Scripture quotations marked NLT are from the *Holy Bible*, New Living Translation, copyright © 1996, 2004. Used by permission of Tyndale House Publishers, Inc., Wheaton, IL 60189. All rights reserved.

Library of Congress Cataloging-in-Publication Data

Connelly, Douglas , 1949–
  Bible prophecy and end times / Douglas Connelly.
    p. cm. – (The indispensable guide to practically everything)
  ISBN 978-0-8249-4772-9
  1. Bible—Prophecies. 2. End of the world. I. Title.
  BS647.3.C66 2009
  236'.9—dc22

                         2009004720

Editor: Lila Empson
Cover and interior design: Whisner Design Group
Typesetting: Educational Publishing Concepts

Printed and bound in the United States of America

10 9 8 7 6 5 4 3 2 1

Only the supernatural mind can have prior knowledge
to the natural mind. If then the Bible has foreknowledge,
historical and scientific, beyond the permutation of
chance . . . it truly then bears the fingerprint of God.

G. B. Hardy

Contents

The Great Disappearance—The Rapture

Terror at Every Turn—The Tribulation

The Last World War—The Battle of Armageddon...... 157

Kingdom Come—The Millennium 181

Judgment Day—Our Accountability to God 205

Prepare for God's arrival! Make the
road smooth and straight!

Matthew 3:3 MSG

Introduction

> [The Bible] tells me that the future is in God's
> hands, and the best is yet to come.
>
> Adrian Rogers

Everyone wants to know the future. Think about your own life—your job, your marriage, your friends, your grades, your kids, your investments. You could have fabulous success and avoid most of life's problems if you could just get a glimpse of what the future holds.

The Bible has a lot to say about the future, but the problem is that prophecy seems to be a confusing mix of different views, strange charts, mysterious visions, and weird symbols. It is just too far-out for most people!

This book is written to help you sort things out with respect to God's plan for the future. It starts with the basics and builds from there. You may feel like a rookie when it comes to prophecy, but you won't stay at that level for long.

Whoever is thirsty, let him come; and whoever wishes, let him take the free gift of the water of life.

Revelation 22:17 NIV

The simple premise of this book is that *God knows the future*. You will be exploring exactly what God has said about future events. Some of what he says is scary; some is fabulous. Some elements in the future are clearly explained; some you will have to piece together from a few hints. But it's all fascinating! The focus will always be on the Bible and what the Bible teaches. This is not an exercise in speculation or daydreaming; it's an exploration of biblical teaching and biblical truth.

Never before has fascination with Bible prophecy been more acute than it is today. Part of that interest is due to the uncertainty of our times. . . . People living in these turbulent times want answers, and many are turning to the Bible to get them.

Tim LaHaye and Ed Hindson

For prophecy to be biblical, it must also be practical. God gave His prophetic truth not just to fill our heads but also to change our hearts.

Charles Swindoll

If you have never studied prophecy and you get confused sometimes by all the jargon Christians throw around, this book will help you figure it all out. Maybe you feel that you know a lot about prophecy, but you've been exposed to only one view about how future events will unfold. This book will take a fair and honest look at all the major approaches to interpreting end-times events.

You may not believe any of this prophecy stuff and you just picked up this book out of curiosity. It's okay if you are not convinced yet! Just approach what is here with an open mind. You may find your life changed by what you read. A fascinating journey lies just ahead!

Then shall the righteous go into everlasting life,
and receive that fullness of joy and refreshing,
which shall come from the presence of the Lord.

The Westminster Confession of Faith

Hallelujah! For the Lord our God,
the Almighty, reigns. Let us rejoice and be glad.

Revelation 19:6–7 NASB

Abraham was confidently looking forward to a city with eternal foundations, a city designed and built by God.

Hebrews 11:10 NLT

The Bible's View of the Future

God, who knows the end from the beginning, has chosen to reveal an amazing amount of information about the future—the world's future and every person's future.

Contents

I am God, and there is none like Me,
declaring the end from the beginning.

Isaiah 46:9–10 NKJV

Prophecy is what God says about the future. He is the only person who knows with absolute certainty what will happen—and he knows it all. Christians trust what God has said in the Bible—his Word—about future events. The Bible doesn't just contain the naive predictions of aspiring fortune-tellers; the Bible records what God knows will happen and what he has planned to happen. God spoke the truth to the Bible's original writers, and he still speaks today through their writings.

You will be amazed at how much of the Bible refers to the future. References to the future are more than just a few obscure verses or a chapter here and there. Prophecy is spread all through the Bible. One respected Bible scholar has calculated that 27 percent of the Bible is prophecy! Prophecy is no minor theme in the Bible. If God put that much in his book, it's clear that he wants his people to understand it and to live in the light of it.

> God will bless everyone who reads this prophecy to others, and he will bless everyone who hears and obeys it. The time is almost here.
>
> Revelation 1:3 CEV
>
> I'm telling you all this ahead of time so that when it happens you will believe that I am who I say I am.
>
> John 13:19 MSG

Jesus certainly took prophecy seriously. He repeatedly pointed to events in his ministry as the fulfillment of Old Testament predictions. Jesus took his own predictions seriously—and he expected his followers would do so as well.

The Bible contains approximately twenty-five hundred predictions about events that were future when the words were recorded or spoken. Two thousand of these predictions have been fulfilled in every detail. (What are the odds?) That means five hundred predictions made in the Bible have yet to be fulfilled—and will be fulfilled as God's program for the future unfolds.

God promises a special blessing to those who study biblical prophecy and seek to live out its implications in their lives (Revelation 1:3). Christians should not be afraid of prophecy or simply dismiss it as too confusing. Biblical prophecy will change your entire perspective on the world around you. Most of all, it will change the way you live!

Digging Deeper

Some biblical books are almost totally predictive prophecy—Zephaniah (89 percent); Nahum (74 percent); Revelation (63 percent). Some of the larger books contain hundreds of verses of prophecy—Ezekiel has 821 verses that speak directly to the future; Isaiah, 754 verses; Matthew, 278 verses. (These calculations all come from J. Barton Payne, *Encyclopedia of Biblical Prophecy* [New York: Harper & Row, 1973].)

What Others Say

To disbelieve or disobey anything a [biblical] prophet says is to disbelieve or disobey God himself.

Wayne Grudem

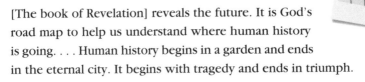

[The book of Revelation] reveals the future. It is God's road map to help us understand where human history is going. . . . Human history begins in a garden and ends in the eternal city. It begins with tragedy and ends in triumph.

Edward Hindson

False or True—Passing the Prophet's Test

God's prophets come on the scene all through the Bible. But God's people also had to contend with *false prophets*—men and women who claimed to speak for God but didn't. Some of the false prophets could have been deluded or mentally unstable, but most were deceivers. They were in the prophet business for profit! They liked being consulted and interviewed. So they claimed to have a word from God, but it was a lie.

✳

False prophets are still around. So God gave his people a series of tests for determining if a prophet was a true one or a false one. (Most of these come from Deuteronomy 13 and 18.) These six tests are a good place to start when someone claims to know the future or to speak with the authority of God:

- Test #1: The true prophet is to speak in the name of the Lord, the true God. A few Christians think it is wise to get everyone's opinion on how the future will unfold and then throw in the Bible for good measure. They play a dangerous game.

- Test #2: The true prophet speaks only at the Lord's command. False prophets use tricks or slick techniques to manipulate the message.

> If the prophet speaks in the Lord's name but his prediction does not happen or come true, you will know that the Lord did not give that message.
>
> Deuteronomy 18:22 NLT
>
> If anyone, regardless of reputation or credentials, preaches something other than what you received originally, let him be cursed.
>
> Galatians 1:9 MSG

- Test #3: A genuine prophet backs up his or her message with a God-honoring life. If an immoral person claims to speak for God, their lifestyle invalidates their message.

- Test #4: The true prophet (sometimes) authenticates the message with a miracle. But an astonishing miracle is never enough to prove that a prophet speaks from God (Deuteronomy 13:1–3).

- Test #5: The true prophet's message is always in harmony with what God has already said in his Word, the Bible.

- Test #6: The true prophet's message *always* comes true. No "two out of three" or "pretty close" in this game.

All the elements have to be in place. If a prophet fails the test at any point, his message is rejected.

Something to Ponder

The Bible warns that false teachers will come from two directions. Some will arise within the Christian community. They will try to make a name for themselves or cash in on gullible Christians. Others will come from outside the Christian community and will bring methods that the Bible rejects—magic, psychic power, access to spirit beings. Christians are to evaluate the prophet's message *and* methods according to the Bible.

Myth Buster

False prophets are often associated with the end times in the Bible. Jesus warned that false prophets and false Christs would come on the scene and would even perform signs and miracles (Mark 13:22). The work of the False Prophet is the work of Satan, who is known for his deceiving character and activity. The apostle Paul even called a false prophet a "child of the devil" (Acts 13:10 NIV).

Prophecy Fulfilled and What Can Be Learned

For Christians, Jesus is everything. It's not surprising, then, that as God unfolds his future plans, Jesus is at the very center of it all. It has always been the case that biblical prophecy centered on Jesus. In the Old Testament, God's prophets spoke of a great Deliverer who would come—an anointed King, the Messiah. What the prophets didn't realize was that the Messiah would come to earth twice—the first time as a humble baby and suffering Savior, the second time as a conquering King.

Some of the best insight for interpreting end-times prophecy comes from studying the prophecies in the Bible about Jesus' *first* coming. For example, the Old Testament prophet Micah predicted that the Messiah would be born in Bethlehem, the same village where King David had been born (Micah 5:2). Seven hundred years later, when Jesus was ready to make his appearance on earth, Mary and Joseph were living in Nazareth (seventy miles from Bethlehem—and a long way to walk!). So God in his providence had a taxation decree issued in Rome at precisely the right time to bring Joseph and Mary to Bethlehem in time for Jesus' birth. The Old Testament prediction was fulfilled *exactly* as the prophets said it would be fulfilled.

It is impossible for God to lie.

Hebrews 6:18 NASB

The entrance of Your words gives light; it gives understanding to the simple.

Psalm 119:130 NKJV

The point is that Christians can expect the biblical prophecies about Jesus' *second* coming to be fulfilled in the same way—exactly the way the prophets spoke them. Because Jesus said that the Son of Man would come in the future on the clouds of heaven, it's safe to conclude that Jesus will actually return bodily to the earth some day.

Jesus is not coming again in some spiritual, allegorical sense. He is literally, visibly returning from heaven. The prophecies not fulfilled in Jesus' first coming still await their fulfillment—in the future, in the wrap-up of human history.

Old Testament Prophecies Fulfilled in Jesus' First Coming

Prophecy About Messiah	Old Testament Prediction	Fulfillment in Jesus
Born of a virgin	Isaiah 7:14	Matthew 1:18–21
Would live in Egypt awhile	Hosea 11:1	Matthew 2:15
Would be a healer	Isaiah 53:4	Matthew 8:16–17
Enter Jerusalem on a donkey	Zechariah 9:9	Matthew 21:4–5
Abandoned by disciples	Zechariah 13:7	Matthew 26:31
Beaten and treated cruelly	Isaiah 50:6	Matthew 26:67; 27:26
Hands and feet pierced	Psalm 22:16; John 19:37	Zechariah 12:10
Soldiers gamble for garments	Psalm 22:18	John 19:23–24
Crucified between two thieves	Isaiah 53:12	Mark 15:27–28
Buried with the rich	Isaiah 53:9	Matthew 27:57–60

Old Testament Prophets You Should Know

Almost every book of the Bible has prophecy in it—some kind of prediction about the future or about an end-time event. A few biblical books, however, are almost completely about future events—future to the writer and future to modern-day readers. You will have a solid start on understanding biblical prophecy if you have some background on these premier prophets. Most of what Christians believe about the future is drawn from these key biblical books.

Daniel

Daniel is the Old Testament point man when it comes to prophecy. You may know him as the man who survived the lions' den, but he has a lot more on his résumé than that. Daniel spent most of his life in the city of Babylon, far from his homeland in Israel. He worked for a succession of pagan Babylonian kings. Sometimes Daniel held positions of honor, and sometimes he was forgotten—until a crisis arose that required the expertise of a person in touch with God.

> I saw One like a son of man coming with the clouds of heaven. He approached the Ancient of Days.
>
> Daniel 7:13 HCSB
>
> A child is born to us, a son is given to us. And the government will rest on his shoulders.
>
> Isaiah 9:6 NLT

Over the years, through visions, dreams, and direct communication, God gave Daniel an incredible amount of information about Israel's future. Some of what God told Daniel came about in the four hundred years that followed Daniel's death. In fact, two-thirds of Daniel's predictions have already been fulfilled—it's ancient history—but that final third is what is so interesting today. The logic in this is easy to follow: If part of Daniel's prophecies happened precisely as he predicted, it is safe to assume that the rest of Daniel's prophecies will take place in the future *just as precisely*.

The final stamp of approval on Daniel's book comes directly from Jesus. He believed that Daniel really existed (he referred to Daniel by name in Matthew 24:15). Jesus even quoted Daniel's writings as an accurate portrayal of events related to Jesus' future return to earth in glory (Mark 14:62 quotes Daniel 7:13).

Daniel has a lot to teach about how God's future plans for Israel and the world will unfold.

Ezekiel

Another key Old Testament player on the prophecy team is Ezekiel. He was a powerful preacher, a creative communicator, and at times was a little weird! He lived in Babylon, as did Daniel, but he didn't minister in the king's palace. Ezekiel's audience was the thousands of Jews who had been deported to Babylon from their homeland of Israel. They were a sad, despondent group, but Ezekiel tried to keep their eyes focused on the awesome majesty of God.

Ezekiel reveals how God will restore his people Israel in the future. What seems spiritually to be a valley of dry bones, dead and unresponsive to God, will miraculously emerge as a new people, filled and energized by God's Spirit. (Ezekiel's most famous vision—the valley of dry bones— is recorded in Ezekiel 37.) Ezekiel also pictures the Messiah's future kingdom and the glorious temple that will be the place of the world's worship during that kingdom (Ezekiel 40–48).

Zechariah

The prophet Zechariah focused on the Messiah's kingdom too. But instead of emphasizing the glory of the kingdom, Zechariah emphasized the glory of the King.

Zechariah lived in Jerusalem after the captives in Babylon returned to their homeland. They returned to a destroyed city and a desolate country. Zechariah's job was to remind the people that God had not forgotten his promises. The Messiah would still come; the Messiah would yet rule over the world.

Other Old Testament Voices

Other Old Testament books that speak at some length about future events include:

• *Isaiah*. The prophet Isaiah lived about one hundred years before Daniel and Ezekiel, but he wrote extensively about the coming Messiah and about the Messiah's kingdom. Many of Isaiah's prophecies related to Jesus' first coming to earth— his birth, his ministry, and his death on the cross.

> He said to me, "Prophesy over these bones: 'Dry bones, listen to the Message of GOD!'"
>
> Ezekiel 37:4 MSG

• *Joel*. The tiny prophecy of Joel touches on the unleashing of the power of the Spirit in the Messiah's kingdom.

• *Zephaniah*. This prophet spoke about the coming of the Lord in majesty and glory and the destruction of Israel's enemies.

• *Psalms*. Even some of the psalms are prophetic and tell us about the Messiah's ultimate victory over evil and the majesty of the coming kingdom.

Something to Ponder

Psalm 22 is one of the prophetic psalms. David gave the reader an unmistakable portrayal of death by crucifixion. The psalm was written long before anyone had been put to death on a cross. Guided by the Holy Spirit, David described the agonizing thirst (v. 15), the

mocking crowd (v. 16), the division of Jesus' garments by the soldiers (v. 18), and the piercing of Jesus' hands and feet (v. 16). The predictions of the psalm were fulfilled one thousand years after David died.

Digging Deeper

The New Testament Gospels cite the writings of Zechariah frequently to demonstrate that Jesus is the Messiah that the Old Testament predicted. Some of Zechariah's predictions were:

• Jesus entering Jerusalem mounted on a donkey (Matthew 21:4-5; Zechariah 9:9).

• Jesus telling his disciples that his enemies will strike the shepherd and scatter the sheep (Matthew 26:31; Zechariah 13:7).

• Jesus pierced with a spear on the cross (John 19:37; Zechariah 12:10).

• Thirty pieces of silver being thrown to the potter (Matthew 27:9; Zechariah 11:12-13).

Something to Ponder

Ezekiel and Joel foretold the coming of God's Spirit to indwell believers in a new and powerful way (Ezekiel 36:26-27; Joel 2:28-29). That prophecy was fulfilled when the Spirit came upon the followers of Jesus on the day of Pentecost—and when the Spirit comes upon those who believe in Jesus today!

Prophetic Books in the New Testament

Many of the books of the New Testament also focus on the future and on end-times prophecy. The book of Revelation is the first one that comes to most people's minds, but large portions of the Gospels are also devoted to prophecy. Segments of prophecy can be found in Paul's letters, in Peter's letters, and in the tiny book of Jude too. Many scholars and students of prophecy have devoted their lives to analyzing and clarifying key sections of biblical prophecy found in the New Testament.

The Gospels

Jesus talked a lot about the future of both the nation of Israel and his new movement called the church. Many of Jesus' parables focused on future events. The Gospels also record some of the Bible's clearest promises about Jesus' return.

> The Revelation of Jesus Christ, which God gave Him to show His servants— things which must shortly take place.
>
> Revelation 1:1 NKJV

> You yourselves know perfectly that the day of the Lord so comes as a thief in the night.
>
> 1 Thessalonians 5:2 NKJV

First and Second Thessalonians

These two letters, written by the apostle Paul, fill in some details about the future that are only hinted at in other biblical books. Key passages about the rapture and the future Antichrist are located in these two New Testament books.

The Book of Revelation

The premier book of the Bible on future events is the book of Revelation. It was written by the apostle John (one of Jesus' closest followers) when he was exiled on the prison island of Patmos. Domitian, the Roman emperor at the time, was trying to wipe out the Christian community, and so he sent John, the last living apostle, into exile. Too bad for Domitian that God had other plans! God gave John a powerful vision of the triumph of Jesus over all evil forever.

This guide is focused on *biblical* prophecy. Don't be intimidated or nervous about that. Even the "experts" struggle with some concepts and some passages of Scripture. The good news is that you can understand most of what Revelation says—or Daniel or Paul or Jesus—and in the process you will learn about what God has in store for *your* future.

Digging Deeper

The word *Apocalypse* (a-pok´-a-lips) is the English spelling of the first Greek word in the original text of the book of Revelation. It means "revealing" or "unveiling." You will sometimes hear the book of Revelation referred to as "the Apocalypse." In modern culture, the word has come to mean a catastrophe or an end-of-the-world event.

Points to Remember

• Several books in both the Old and the New Testaments focus on prophecy—future events from God's perspective.

• Some things in these books are difficult to understand, but they are difficult for *everyone*!

• God wants his people to understand the plans he has for the world's future.

Jesus' Teaching on the Future

One of the longest sermons Jesus gave about the future is recorded in Matthew 24 and 25. (Shorter versions of the same sermon appear in Mark 13 and Luke 21.) The sermon is called the Olivet Discourse because Jesus spoke the words on the Mount of Olives, looking down on the city of Jerusalem. Like all biblical prophecy, Christians have interpreted Jesus' sermon in different ways. Exploring those differences will help you begin to grasp some of the essential truths of end-times prophecy.

The "In the Past" View

Some Christians believe that the prophecies Jesus spoke in AD 30 were fulfilled completely forty years later in AD 70 when the Roman armies destroyed the city of Jerusalem. The signs of the times that Jesus predicted would come—tribulation, false messiahs, wars, persecution, apostasy—accompanied the failed Jewish revolt against the Romans in AD 66–73.

> You will hear of wars and threats of wars, but don't panic. Yes, these things must take place, but the end won't follow immediately.
>
> Matthew 24:6 NLT
>
> The Son of Man will be seen coming in the clouds with great power and glory.
>
> Mark 13:26 CEV

Two key elements in the Olivet Discourse lead people to this position. First, Jesus promised that "this generation will certainly not pass away until all these things have happened" (Matthew 24:34; Mark 13:30; Luke 21:32 NIV). Jesus' words seem to say that some of the people in that first generation of Christians would be alive when all the things he predicted would come true.

The second element that undergirds this position is the view that Jesus' "coming," promised in the Olivet Discourse, was not his return in power but his coming against Israel in judgment. God was demonstrating that the old order of the Law was passing off the scene, and the new order of the church was now in place. In this view, the "coming" of Christ and the great tribulation have already occurred.

The Future View

The second major position on interpreting the Olivet Discourse is the futurist view, a widely held view, particularly among American Christians. This view teaches that the signs of the times in Jesus' sermon herald a time of tribulation that is yet to come on the world. Those who hold this view believe the Olivet Discourse predicted the unfolding of the end times in three stages:

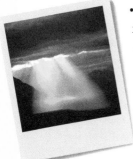

• Matthew 24:4–14 reflects events in the first half of the future seven-year tribulation. These are the beginning of God's judgments on the earth. The earthquakes, famines, and wars are not referring to events in this present age, but to events during the early part of the tribulation. This time will also see a rise in false prophets and wickedness, along with the worldwide preaching of the gospel.

• Matthew 24:15–28 reflects events in the second half of the tribulation. This period begins with the desecration of the temple by the Antichrist and the subsequent persecution of the Jewish people. It will also be a time of devastating judgment on the earth. Jesus said that if this time was not cut short and limited to three and a half years, no one would survive.

• Matthew 24:29–31 describes the second coming of Christ in power. This event will be witnessed by all humanity. When Jesus returns, the Antichrist and his armies will be destroyed, and Jesus will establish his kingdom on earth.

The Already—Not Yet View

The third view of the prophecies of the Olivet Discourse sees the first half of the sermon as having been fulfilled at the fall of Jerusalem in AD 70 (the "already" aspect), while the second half of the discourse awaits final completion at the second coming of Jesus in the future (the "not yet" aspect). According to this view, the destruction of Jerusalem in the past serves as a preview of the future tribulation. The signs of the times that began in Jesus' generation—wars, rumors of wars, earthquakes, persecution—will continue in some form in every generation until Jesus returns.

> When all this starts to happen, up on your feet. Stand tall with your heads high. Help is on the way!
>
> Luke 21:28 MSG

The second chapter of Matthew's version of Jesus' sermon centers around three parables that relate to the future. The first parable, the story of the ten bridesmaids (Matthew 25:1-13), was a challenge to be ready for the Lord's return. The second parable, a story of three servants (Matthew 25:14-30), spoke to the master's rewards to those who are faithful while he is away. The third parable, the story of the sheep and the goats (Matthew 25:31-46), focused on the final judgment in which Jesus separates out those who have refused to believe in him.

Digging Deeper

Matthew, the author of the first Gospel in the arrangement of the New Testament, records more of Jesus' predictions about the future than any of the other Gospel writers. Matthew was one of Jesus' closest followers during his ministry, so he was writing down the things he had heard directly from Jesus. Matthew wrote to present Jesus as the King—and Christians learn in his Gospel how to live as loyal subjects of the King. Matthew also focused

on the kingdom in his Gospel—the kingdom today and the kingdom yet to come.

Something to Ponder

In Mark's version of Jesus' prophetic sermon, the first word Jesus spoke was "watch" (Mark 13:5 NIV). In Greek the word means to "be discerning." The last word of the discourse (in Greek) is another word translated "watch"—a word meaning "be alert and faithful." The overall message of Mark 13 seems to be that since no one knows when the end will come, vigilance is required every moment. Testing and trials will come, but the faithful follower of Jesus will be hard at work when Jesus returns.

Final Thoughts

How watchful are you? Does the fact that Jesus may return at any moment ever cross your mind in the course of a week or a month? The promise of Jesus' "any moment" return might make a big difference in what you watch this week or where you spend your time.

What About Nostradamus?

Michel de Notredame (1503–1566), more popularly known as Nostradamus, was a French physician who developed an interest in astrology and prophecy. He wrote a series of four-line verses and arranged them in ten books of one hundred verses each. His book, titled *Centuries*, claims to predict events from his time until the year 3797. Here's one of his four-line prophecies: "The young lion will overcome the old one, / On the field of battle in a single combat; / He will put out his eyes in a cage of gold; / Two fleets one, then to die, a cruel death."

Nostradamus's verses are not in any chronological order. They jump back and forth throughout history, supposedly prophesying events at different points in time. His predictions, however, are couched in obscure phrases and symbols and can be interpreted pretty much according to the whims of the reader.

Nostradamus further complicates matters by not dating any of his prophecies. When the two World Trade Center towers were attacked and collapsed in September of

Dear friends, do not believe every spirit, but test the spirits to determine if they are from God, because many false prophets have gone out into the world.

1 John 4:1 HCSB

Satan himself transforms himself into an angel of light.

2 Corinthians 11:14 NKJV

2001, supporters of Nostradamus found what they thought was a clear prediction of that event in one line that read, "The twins will fall." Most of Nostradamus's predictions "fit" only after the event when a suitable line or two of his writings can be pulled out and applied to the situation. James Randi, author of *The Mask of Nostradamus*, claims that in the 103 cases in which Nostradamus specifically mentions identifiable persons or dates, he was wrong 100 percent of the time!

Nostradamus reflected the secularism of the French Renaissance. Before his time, almost all end-times thinkers had expected that God would bring an end to the world. Nostradamus focused on a secular end to human history. He thought humankind would wipe itself out by war or disease. Nostradamus never spoke of divine judgment, heaven, or hell.

There is no real comparison between Nostradamus's predictions and those of the Bible. His are vague and fallible. Even his most ardent supporters admit that many of his predictions were wrong. The prophecies of the Bible, however, are clear and infallible.

Myth Buster

On May 6, 1981, the *USA Today* newspaper warned that Nostradamus had predicted a massive earthquake would hit California on May 10. But no earthquake came four days later. As a matter of fact, Nostradamus mentioned no country, city, or year. He spoke only of a "rumbling earth" in a "new city" and a "very mighty quake" on May 10—but no year! Most of the prophecies of Nostradamus are just that vague and unclear. If an earthquake hits sometime on May 10, someone will hail Nostradamus as a great prophet!

Digging Deeper

Nostradamus admitted in his writings that he relied on demonic power and occult practices for his prophecies. One of Nostradamus's supporters claims that magic, astrology, and black angels are keys to understanding the source and interpretation of his predictions. Those assertions alone should be enough for Christians to  avoid such false prophets as accurate or dependable predictors of future events. The apostle John challenged Christians to "test" the spirits, not to "believe" the spirits (1 John 4:1). Just because a person claims to be a prophet does not mean that Christians should trust their predictions.

What's a Prophet to Do?

In Bible times, God selected certain men and women to speak his message. They didn't come up with their own agenda; they spoke God's truth even when no one was willing to listen. The messengers who spoke about future events were called *prophets* or *prophetesses*. They spoke for someone else. They didn't represent a political leader or a wealthy businessperson but the Lord God. God moved some of the prophets to write down their messages, and they are preserved in the Bible for everyone to read. The key point is: prophets spoke God's message about the future.

Sometimes the prophets spoke about *their own immediate future*. God would tell the prophet which side would win a battle or what judgment would fall on a disobedient king. David was Israel's greatest king, but he had committed adultery and then plotted murder to keep his sin a secret. God sent Nathan the prophet to David to confront the king with his sin (2 Samuel 12). Good news or bad news, the prophet had to speak what God told him.

 The last words of David . . . "The Spirit of the LORD spoke by me, and His word was on my tongue."

2 Samuel 23:1–2 NASB

The LORD touched my mouth and said, "See, I have put my words in your mouth!"

Jeremiah 1:9 NLT

At other times the prophets predicted events *that were fulfilled hundreds of years later*. Isaiah lived seven centuries before Jesus was born, and yet, under God's direction, Isaiah painted a vivid portrait of Jesus death on the cross (Isaiah 53).

Some of the predictions of biblical prophets have *yet to happen*. Isaiah pictured a world of peace in which the wolf and the lamb will lie down together and children will play safely near a cobra's den (Isaiah 11:6–9). The prophet Amos predicted a time of such prosperity on earth that people gathering food from a field one day will be followed by people planting a new crop the next day (Amos 9:13). The apostle John in the New Testament says that God in judgment will hurl something like a huge fiery mountain into the sea, and a third of the sea will turn to blood (Revelation 8:8–9).

Since God's words to the prophets about past events came true, the prophet's predictions about future events can be trusted completely.

Myth Buster

During the 1960s and 1970s Jeane Dixon became a legend, primarily because she had predicted in *Parade* magazine in 1950 that John F. Kennedy would be elected president and then would die in office. But here are some of her other predictions:

- World War III would start in 1954.

- Russia would be the first nation to land humans on the moon.

- Jackie Kennedy would never remarry. (She married Aristotle Onassis the day *after* Dixon's prediction!)

Points to Remember

- Prophets and prophetesses spoke in place of someone else. They spoke God's message, not their own.

- Prophets had two primary roles: *forth-telling* what God was doing in the world and foretelling future events.

Where Christians Disagree About the Future

If you talk to Christian friends or pick up a few books on biblical prophecy, it won't take you long to figure out that there are many different views on how the future will unfold. The disagreements don't arise so much from what the Bible actually says as from how various traditions approach biblical prophecy as a whole. Within the Christian community all these views (and combinations of views) exist and even thrive. Books are written, seminars are held, sermons are preached—all defending one position or another.

⁂

Some Christians take a *literal* approach to prophecy. The Old Testament predictions about the Messiah that were not fulfilled in Jesus' first coming will be fulfilled at Jesus' second coming—and just as literally as the prophecies of his first coming. For example, since the Old Testament promises the nation of Israel that the Messiah will reign in Jerusalem over a worldwide kingdom, these Christians believe that the kingdom is still to come—and that it will be exactly like the Old Testament prophecies picture it to be.

Anyone with ears to hear must listen to the Spirit and understand what he is saying to the churches.

Revelation 3:22 NLT

"Do you understand what you're reading?" He answered, "How can I without some help?"

Acts 8:30–31 MSG

Other Christians take a different approach. These Christians contend that, because Israel rejected Jesus as her Messiah, those Old Testament prophecies have been transferred from Israel to the church, the New Testament people of God. Therefore, for example, Christians are not to look for an earthly, literal kingdom, as Old Testament Israel did. Those promises are now fulfilled spiritually in Jesus Christ and in the church. In this view, prophecy is not to be taken so literally. Look instead for the *spiritual* meaning.

Still other Christians say that prophecy is to be interpreted in the context of the ongoing conflict between good and evil. The symbols of prophetic visions are meant to point to *larger truths* that affect people in every age. The "big picture" of prophecy is to show Christians that Christ will ultimately triumph over all his enemies. Instead of wrangling about whether there is an earthly kingdom or not, Christians should be living each day under Christ's lordship.

Something to Ponder

One older approach to the biblical prophecy was called the "historicist" view. Those who held this position taught that the book of Revelation reveals an outline of human history throughout the church age. One advocate, Alexander Hardie, wrote this in 1926: "The last Great War of 1914–1918, which convulsed and disgraced humanity, was doubtless the predicted [battle of] Armageddon." His view was undoubtedly revised when World War II came along twenty years later.

Points to Remember

Several principles to keep in mind when it comes to the debates over biblical prophecy:

- *Have a position.* Come to a place of personal conviction on the issues of prophecy.

- *Hold that position with humility.* Bible-believing, Christ-honoring Christians hold other views. Respect them.

- *Keep discussions on the level of issues rather than personalities.* Keep the focus on what the Bible says.

What Christians All Agree On

Whenever the topic of biblical prophecy comes up, it seems all the emphasis is on where Christians disagree. They hold different views on when Jesus will come back and on what the kingdom of God will look like and who the seven-headed Beast in Revelation 13 represents. Isn't there something about end-times prophecy that Christians can agree on? Actually, Christians are in amazing agreement on some of the "big" issues related to prophecy and the future. It's just that these things sometimes get lost in the debates over the issues where they disagree.

Christians who honor the Bible as God's truth have at least six broad areas of agreement when it comes to God's plan for the future.

- *God created human beings to live forever.* Christians believe that human beings live on beyond the point of physical death. The body may die, but the human spirit or soul lives on. Human beings are not absorbed back into the universe. Human beings do not become angels or find themselves reincarnated as a different form of life. They live on after death as essentially the same beings they were here on earth. Human beings were designed by God to be immortal.

> May the God of endurance and encouragement grant you agreement with one another, according to Christ Jesus, so that you may glorify . . . God.
>
> Romans 15:5–6 HCSB
>
> [There is] one Lord, one faith, one baptism; one God and Father of all, who is above all, and through all, and in you all.
>
> Ephesians 4:5–6 NKJV

- *Human beings experience conscious existence between physical death and the resurrection of the body.* Christians believe that at death those people who have believed in Jesus in this life enter a state of rest and joy in the presence of Jesus. Those who

41

have refused to believe in Jesus enter a state of separation from him. Human beings are consciously aware of where they are and what is going on around them. They can act and speak and react to other people in the afterlife and to God.

• *The bodies of human beings will be raised from the dead.* All human beings, whether believers or unbelievers, will be raised from the dead. Their bodies may "sleep" in the grave or totally decompose into the earth, but some day God will call that body back into existence. Their conscious spirits will in the future be reunited with resurrected bodies. The bodies of believers in Jesus will experience the resurrection to life in bodies designed for eternity. Sin, pain, and disease will be gone forever. The bodies of unbelievers will experience the resurrection to judgment before God.

• *All human beings will stand before God to give an account of their lives.* Unbelievers will simply hear God's sentence of separation from him. They will be without excuse for their rejection of God's gift of salvation. Believers in Jesus will give an account too. Their lives will be evaluated and rewarded according to the faithfulness of their obedience to Jesus Christ.

• *Jesus will return.* All Christians agree that Jesus will return to earth a second time. The Bible is so clear on the *fact* of Jesus' return that there is no real debate about it.

• *An eternal heaven is prepared for those who believe in Jesus as Savior; eternal separation from Jesus will be the destiny of those who refuse God's grace.* There is no disagreement among Christians that every human being will experience eternity. Christians look for a new heaven and a new earth of peace and joy forever.

On the big items, all Christians are in agreement! It doesn't matter what your denomination or tradition is; these six issues are part of your belief system. All Christians also agree that the Bible contains a number of prophecies that have yet to be fulfilled. Disagreement comes with respect to the sequence and timing and nature of some of those events,

> Among us you are all equal. That is, we are all in a common relationship with Jesus Christ.
>
> Galatians 3:28 MSG

but the events themselves are certain. You will find more views and more variations in this book than you thought possible, but don't lose sight of the basic agreement of Christians on the issues that really matter. Every Christian should hold and defend his or her position, but keep the disagreements in proper perspective.

Some day God will do his work of bringing human history to an end, and every believer will have to agree on one more issue: God will be proven in every issue to be right, and every Christian will be shown (to some degree) to be wrong.

Something to Ponder

It's easy to assume that the early Christians were in agreement on everything, but that isn't the case. Paul and Barnabas disagreed on whether they should take Mark with them on their second preaching journey. Barnabas said yes; Paul said no. They ended up going two different directions—and preaching about Jesus in

twice as many places! Paul knew that some Christians disagreed with him on some points, but his main concern was that they preach the true message (Philippians 1:14-18). Personal issues were never to stand in the way of telling people about God's love and grace.

Points to Remember

- Christians agree on the big issues about God's plan for the future.

- Christians disagree on the time sequence of events or on how prophecy is to be interpreted, but those disagreements are not to create a spirit of division or judgment.

What Others Say

Deliver us from ignorance, error, lovelessness, pride, selfishness, impurity, and cowardice. Enable us to be truthful, kind, humble, sympathetic, pure, and courageous.

The Amsterdam Declaration 2000

There is simply no place in the family of God for name calling, false accusation, slander, evil insinuations, and guilt-by-association techniques. God forgive us all of such sins.

Robert Lightner

None of us dare sing the third verse of "Onward, Christian Soldiers" without a heartfelt prayer for forgiveness. We sing:

We are not divided, all one body we,
One in hope and doctrine, one in charity . . .
But we are divided.

James Boice

That which enables us to know and understand aright in the things of God must be a living principle of holiness within us.

John Smith

Handling the Tough Passages

Prophecy in the Bible is not easy reading. Some of it is pretty difficult to read and even more difficult to understand—and only *God* has the answers on some passages. But there are a few guidelines for finding your way around. These basic principles will help you keep your feet on solid ground. If you ever get lost, come back to these home base coordinates on the map. They will always lead you back to safe ground.

✳

• *Always read a prophetic statement in the context in which it was given.* Look around when you read prophecy. Who is speaking? Who is listening? What hints are there in the passage about the time frame?

• *Find out what other Scripture passages say about the same event or person.* For example, the apostle Paul talked about a lawless man who will be revealed in the future (2 Thessalonians 2:3–4). A reference Bible will indicate that Revelation 13 is a passage that will give you more insight on the identity of that person. Try to find all the pieces of a prediction and get the whole picture.

Open my eyes so that I may see wonderful things in Your law.

Psalm 119:18 HCSB

The word of God is living and active and sharper than any two-edged sword . . . able to judge the thoughts and intentions of the heart.

Hebrews 4:12 NASB

• *Don't be put off by symbols or vivid imagery.* Some people read about a Beast coming out of the sea with ten horns and seven heads (Revelation 13:1)—and they close the book! Remember that the symbols are not literally true, but they represent aspects of the prophecy that are literally true. The seven heads of the Beast, for example, represent seven nations or political entities.

- *Try to read and interpret biblical prophecy in its normal sense.* Obviously a seven-headed Beast rising out of the sea needs some explanation beyond the literal sense of the words. Figures of speech are common in everyday language. The Bible uses figures of speech too—and allegories and metaphors and parables and riddles—but be careful not to read in a hidden meaning when no hidden meaning is implied or necessary.

Something to Ponder

 The study of biblical prophecy leads down some dark roads and through some dreadful days—but don't lose heart! God can reveal what will happen because he knows it all and has planned it all. And he knows how the story ends!

Further Insights

Vivid, figurative speech is not used only in the prophetic sections of the Bible:

- The prophet Amos did not say "God is mad"; he wrote "The lion has roared" (Amos 3:8 NIV).

- Jesus pointed to himself as the good shepherd (John 10:11), the true vine (John 15:1), and the light of the world (John 9:5).

- Isaiah did not write a dry discourse on sin and forgiveness. He used figurative language that his readers never forget: "If your sins are blood-red, they'll be snow-white" (Isaiah 1:18 MSG).

Prophecy's Big Picture Is Jesus

With so much information in the Bible about end-times prophecy, most people don't even know where to start! Those who are interested in prophecy want to jump right in talking about the mark of the Beast or how long the tribulation will last or who the Antichrist might be. (If you aren't familiar with those terms, don't panic. You will understand them soon enough.) As fascinating as some of those subjects are, the place to begin is with the central, most important, most universally known prediction in the Bible: Jesus said, "I'll come back" (John 14:3 MSG).

That promise is the bottom line of everything Christians believe about the future. All other prophecy revolves around and springs from this clear prediction that Jesus, who lived here on earth, died on the cross, and rose from the dead—this same Jesus—will come back again.

Jesus himself clearly predicted his second coming several times during his ministry on earth—and the other New Testament writers were just as convinced of the certainty that Jesus would come again. The *fact* of his coming is never in doubt. Jesus will return at the Father's appointed time. While scoffers may question the reality of his return and mock Christians for believing it for two thousand years, the delay reveals God's patience and his desire that many will come to repentance and faith (2 Peter 3:4, 8-9).

> He who testifies about these things says, "Yes, I am coming quickly." Amen! Come, Lord Jesus!
>
> Revelation 22:20 HCSB
>
> Scoffers will come in the last days, walking according to their own lusts, and saying, "Where is the promise of His coming?"
>
> 2 Peter 3:3–4 NKJV

The Bible not only makes the promise of Jesus' return clear; it also makes the responsibility of every Christian clear. Believers are to be spiritually alert and prepared. They are to be watchful, expecting the Lord's coming at any moment.

Christians wait for the "blessed hope"—the glorious appearing of the great God and Savior, Jesus Christ (Titus 2:13 NKJV). If nothing else, the study of biblical prophecy should bring you to a place of deeper joy and greater anticipation that Jesus will soon return.

Digging Deeper

The word *Messiah* in Hebrew means "the Anointed One." It is a title for Jesus that is used in relation to the people of Israel. Jesus is God's great Deliverer who would deliver Israel (and all who would believe in him) from the condemnation of sin through his sacrifice on the cross. The New Testament (Greek) term for Messiah is *the Christ*. Jesus is his name; Christ is his title.

Something to Ponder

Not every Christian feels comfortable praying, "Come, Lord Jesus." It's pretty comfortable in this world. Maybe if Christians prayed that little prayer more often— "Come, Lord Jesus"—they would focus more on what really matters in the here and now.

The Great Disappearance—
The Rapture

A great event could occur at any moment! Jesus could return in the clouds for his people—and take them instantly to heaven.

Contents

We will all be changed, in a moment,
in the twinkling of an eye.

1 Corinthians 15:51–52 NASB

What the Rapture Is All About

You have probably seen the bumper sticker: "In Case of Rapture, This Vehicle Will Be Without a Driver!" Okay—but what does that mean?

The rapture is a future event predicted in the Bible in which Jesus will return from heaven, gather his followers, and take them directly to heaven. If you've never heard of the rapture, it sounds a little weird, but you should know that Christians didn't just dream this up. Christians believe in the rapture because the Bible clearly teaches that such an event will happen.

✠

The apostle Paul is the New Testament writer who provides the most detail about the rapture. His teaching arose from a very practical problem in one of the Christian communities he had founded. Paul had gone to the city of Thessalonica and had preached about Jesus—and a group of people had believed. Paul was able to stay only a few weeks with these people, but he told them about Jesus' return. The problem arose after Paul left. A few of the older Christians in the community died. That made the other believers wonder about what would happen to those friends. Would they be left out of the glory of Jesus' return?

The Lord Himself will descend from heaven with a shout, with the archangel's voice, and with the trumpet of God.

1 Thessalonians 4:16 HCSB

Let me tell you something wonderful, a mystery I'll probably never fully understand. We're not all going to die—but we are all going to be changed. You hear a blast to end all blasts from a trumpet, and in the time that you look up and blink your eyes—it's over.

1 Corinthians 15:51–52 MSG

Paul assured them in 1 Thessalonians 4:13–18 that those who had died would not be left behind. When Jesus comes back he will bring back with him all those who have died. Their bodies, which have been buried and may have even crumbled to dust, will be resurrected and changed. They will have a body like Jesus' body—a body built for eternity. Those Christians still alive on earth at the moment of Jesus' return will be changed too—and then caught up to meet Jesus in the air.

That event described in 1 Thessalonians 4—Jesus' return in the air for his people—is the rapture.

Something to Ponder

 We will not all sleep" (NIV). That surprising statement by the apostle Paul in 1 Corinthians 15:51 contains the promise that one generation of believers will not experience physical death. Christians who are still alive when Jesus returns will not die, but will be "caught up" (raptured) and instantly changed. Christians will be taken out of this world into heaven to be with Jesus and other believers forever.

Digging Deeper

You won't find the word *rapture* anywhere in the Bible! The word comes from a Latin translation of 1 Thessalonians 4:16-17. In verse 17 the words "caught up" (NIV) were translated *rapturo* in the Latin Bible—and, with use, the word morphed into the English word *rapture*. It is a word Christians use to describe a biblical event.

When Will It Happen?

Christians are in basic agreement on the *fact* of the rapture, but there are several different views on when the rapture will take place

If you have been exposed to only one view in your church or in your reading, you might be surprised by how many views there are. You might also be surprised by how many Christians hold views different from the one you hold. While there are clear statements in the Bible about *what* the rapture will be like, there is no clear, definitive statement about *when* it will occur.

It really isn't accurate to say that Christians have decided when the rapture will take place. The best that students of biblical prophecy can do is try to place the rapture in a framework of future events—to figure out when it will happen *in* relation to other events.

The main question about the time of the rapture is when it will occur in relation to the tribulation. Many Christians believe that at the end of our present age, a period of distress will come on the world for seven years—a time of tribulation. (This event is discussed in detail in the section "Terror at Every Turn.") The issue prophecy students struggle

Don't you be slovenly and careless. Just when you don't expect him, the Son of Man will show up.

Luke 12:40 MSG

You know quite well that the day of the Lord's return will come unexpectedly, like a thief in the night.

1 Thessalonians 5:2 NLT

with is this: Will Jesus return to rescue his followers before the tribulation or at the end or somewhere in the middle?

Each of these possibilities will be explored in this chapter. You should keep in mind that each view on the time of the rapture is based on hints and clues drawn from the Bible, but no one can point to a Scripture verse that says exactly when Jesus will come in relation to the tribulation. Some views may have a stronger biblical foundation than others, but no single view answers every question about the timing of the rapture. In the end, you will have to decide which view you think is most consistent with the biblical evidence.

Myth Buster

If someone comes along and says he knows *the date* of Jesus' return, put that book back on the shelf, turn to another television channel, or click on a new Web site. The Bible says that *no one* knows the exact time, date, season, or year of Jesus' return. When he was on earth, Jesus himself didn't even know the date of his return! Here's what he said: "The exact day and hour? No one knows that, not even heaven's angels, not even the Son. Only the Father knows" (Matthew 24:36 MSG).

Something to Ponder

• The rapture is an event predicted in the Bible in which Jesus will return from heaven and take all Christians, living and dead, to be with him forever.

• The Bible tells us that no one (except the Father) knows the precise time of Jesus' return. Don't be duped by someone who claims to have it all figured out.

• Christians agree on the *fact* of Jesus' return but disagree on *when* the rapture will occur in relation to other future events.

Rapture Timeline One: Jesus Will Come at the End of the Tribulation

Some Christians have looked at the biblical evidence and concluded that believers in Jesus will go through the entire tribulation. This position is called the (you guessed it!) "posttribulation rapture" view.

The future scenario, according to posttribulationists, looks like this:

- The world will continue its downward spiral until God brings his judgment in the form of seven years of great tribulation.

- Christians will increasingly be persecuted through the tribulation until Jesus returns to rescue his faithful people in the rapture.

- Then all of God's church, all the Christians of every generation, will return to earth immediately with Jesus in victory.

> Immediately after the tribulation of those days: The sun will be darkened, and the moon will not shed its light; the stars will fall from the sky, and the celestial powers will be shaken. Then the sign of the Son of Man will appear in the sky, and then all the peoples of the earth will mourn; and they will see the Son of Man.
>
> Matthew 24:29–30 HCSB

> As it was in the days of Noah, so it will be also in the days of the Son of Man.
>
> Luke 17:26 NKJV

✶

Posttributionists make some good arguments for their position—but not everyone agrees!

Posttrib Strengths

1. The Bible indicates that Christians will experience serious persecution and suffering in the present age. Jesus said, "In this world

you will have trouble. But take heart! I have overcome the world" (John 16:33 NIV). Or how about these words from Paul and Barnabas: "Through many tribulations we must enter the kingdom of God" (Acts 14:22 NASB). These verses clearly show that Christians will experience the times of tribulation that will come on the world in the future.

2. Jesus said that he would allow some Christians to experience great tribulation: "Do not fear what you are about to suffer. . . . You will have tribulation for ten days" (Revelation 2:10 NASB).

3. The Bible's promises that we will be rescued from God's wrath refer only to God's *eternal* judgment on sin. We *will* be delivered from the eternal penalty of sin but not from suffering on earth at the hands of God's enemies.

4. Jesus taught that Christians would be on earth when the Antichrist appears during the tribulation (Mark 13:14–23). Jesus also pointed to his return in glory at the end of the tribulation as the event that Christians should be looking for (Mark 13:26, 35).

5. Some passages of Scripture seem to imply that the New Testament writers did not expect Jesus to return at any moment. Jesus told Peter that Peter would die in his old age (John 21:18-19). Some of Jesus' parables and other teachings suggest that a long period of time will intervene between Jesus' first coming and his second coming (Matthew 13:1-50; Luke 19:11-27).

Some Contrary Posttrib Views

The posttribulation rapture view has also come under the scrutiny of Christians who hold different views. They raise some interesting points:

1. Scripture's statements about the church experiencing tribulation or suffering refer to times of persecution or opposition that Christians have endured throughout the entire span of time since Jesus was here. Those statements are not referring to the final tribulation period.

2. The posttribulation rapture view contradicts the biblical teaching that Jesus could return for his followers at any moment. If Jesus won't come until the end of the seven-year tribulation, Christians at some point will be able to calculate very closely when he will return.

3. The parables that imply a long period of time between Jesus' first coming and his second coming also contain warnings about being ready for his return at any moment. Jesus' prediction about Peter's old age did not rule out Jesus' return at any moment. The prediction could still have been fulfilled in God's plan.

4. Jesus' teaching about the Antichrist in the Gospels was given to his disciples before the New Testament teaching about the rapture was made clear. Jesus did not explain how the events would unfold. Christians have to merge the New Testament teaching that the rapture will take place at any moment with the things that Jesus taught in the Gospels.

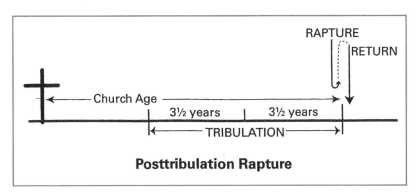

Posttribulation Rapture

Something to Ponder

Three views. Each one is held by sincere Christians who base their conclusions on the Bible. There's only one problem. Who's right?

The best approach is to examine the biblical evidence for each view and then come to your own conclusion. But instead of arguing about the different views with other Christians, keep your focus on the central truth: Jesus *is* coming back—and Christians are called to live every moment in that light.

Digging Deeper

The Greek word translated "caught up" in 1 Thessalonians 4:17 is used a total of fourteen times in the New Testament with three senses: (1) "to steal or carry away" (Matthew 12:29; John 10:12); (2) "to lead away by force" (Matthew 11:12; 13:19; John 6:1-5; 10:28-29; Acts 23:10; Jude 23); and (3) "to be carried away by the Holy Spirit" (Acts 8:39; 2 Corinthians 12:2, 4; Revelation 12:5). It is in this final sense that the word is used to refer to the catching away of Christians at the time of Jesus' return.

Points to Remember

• Christians agree that Jesus will return some day; they disagree on how his return will fit with other future events.

• The key "sticking point" is the relationship between the rapture and the future tribulation period.

• Examine the biblical evidence and come to your own solid conclusion about the rapture—but realize that committed Christians hold differing viewpoints.

Rapture Timeline Two: Jesus Will Come in the Middle of the Tribulation

This view of when the rapture will take place is called the "midtribulation rapture" view or the "prewrath rapture." Here's how events unfold in this version of the future:

- Christians will experience part of the tribulation— probably the first three and a half years of the seven-year tribulation.

- At about the midpoint of the tribulation, Jesus will return in the air and take Christians out of the world.

- Those people who are left on earth during the last half of the tribulation will experience God's wrath. At the end of the tribulation, Jesus will return in power to set up his kingdom of peace.

As with the other views, there are pros and cons to the view that Jesus will return for his people in the middle or near the middle of the tribulation.

Arguments in Favor

Those Christians who believe that Jesus will come during the tribulation base their position on the following evidence:

1. Jesus promised that the time of tribulation would be shortened for his followers (Matthew 24:21-22). In order to preserve genuine believers, Jesus said that the amount of time they will experience God's judgment will be shortened by the rapture.

> It will happen in a moment, in the blink of an eye, when the last trumpet is blown. For when the trumpet sounds, those who have died will be raised to live forever. And we who are living will also be transformed . . . into bodies that will never die.
>
> 1 Corinthians 15:52–53 NLT

2. The Bible promises that Christians will be delivered from God's *wrath*, not from the tribulation itself. Since the seven bowl judgments in Revelation are specifically called "the seven bowls of God's wrath" (Revelation 16:1 NIV), Christians are raptured just *before* the bowl judgments begin. (This is where the phrase "prewrath rapture" comes from.)

3. Paul said in 1 Corinthians 15:52 that the rapture would take place "at the last trumpet" (NIV). The last trumpet judgment will occur in the middle of the tribulation, so that seems to be the precise time that Jesus will come for his people.

4. The church *is* pictured on earth during the tribulation. In Revelation 11:4, John referred to two lampstands that stand before the  Lord of the earth. In Revelation 1:20, churches are called lampstands, and it seems reasonable to conclude that the lampstands in Revelation 11 also represent churches. The two lampstands in Revelation 11 will be attacked but then will be taken up to heaven in a cloud (Revelation 11:12). This seems like a clear reference to the rapture, and it takes place in the middle of the tribulation—not before it begins and not at the end.

Arguments Against

Christians who hold other views have raised some serious questions about the midtrib/prewrath position.

1. The *entire* seven-year period of the tribulation is referred to as the time of God's wrath. Revelation 6:16–17 describes a time early in the tribulation when people of the earth cry out for the rocks and mountains to fall on them. The passage clearly refers to that time of judgment as the great day of God's wrath.

2. Paul's reference to "the last trumpet" (1 Corinthians 15:52 NIV) means the trumpet call that will accompany the rapture, *not* the seventh trumpet judgment in the middle of the tribulation. (Check out 1 Thessalonians 4:16 and Revelation 4:1.)

3. The two lampstands in Revelation 11 refer to two human beings, not churches. These two witnesses for God during the tribulation are slain by the Antichrist but are raised to life by God and then are taken to heaven (Revelation 11:7–12). *They* are removed in the middle of the tribulation, not all Christian believers.

The midtribulation rapture view was once a widely held view among Bible teachers and Christians in general. Then it entered a season of decline, particularly as the teaching of the Scofield Reference Bible took hold among Christians in the early twentieth century. C. I. Scofield was a pastor and teacher who vigorously taught the pretribulation rapture. In the last few decades, the midtribulation or prewrath rapture view has seen a resurgence of popularity—and it has sparked a whole new round of discussion and debate among students of biblical prophecy.

> Fear nothing in the things you're about to suffer— but stay on guard! Fear nothing! The Devil is about to throw you in jail for a time of testing—ten days. It won't last forever.
>
> Revelation 2:10 MSG

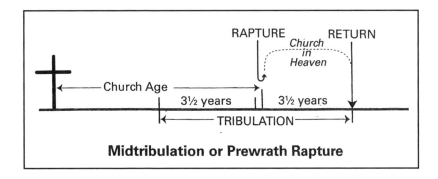

Midtribulation or Prewrath Rapture

Myth Buster

Several researchers claim to have found astonishing messages hidden in the Bible. The basic belief is that there are hidden codes in the Hebrew text of the Old Testament. Computers are used to scan the letters that appear at specific intervals—every three letters, for example—and the results are examined for words or names. Bible code researchers claim to have found references to Hitler, John Kennedy, and even New York City. What they don't tell you is that researchers have also found more than two thousand references to Muhammad—and one hundred references to Krishna, a Hindu god.

Something to Ponder

The word *tribulation* is used in the Bible in a general sense to mean "troubles" or "suffering" or "hardships." But the word is also used to describe a specific time of distress that God will allow to sweep over the world. It will not be a pleasant time for anyone on the earth.

Digging Deeper

The midtribulation rapture view attempts to take advantage of elements in both the pretribulation and posttribulation views. With those who believe the rapture will come *before* the tribulation, midtribulationists argue for two aspects to Christ's second coming—the rapture and Christ's return in glory. They also believe (like pretribulationists) that the rapture is a physical event, an actual removal of believers from earth. With the posttribulation view, those who hold to a middle-of-the-tribulation view believe that the church will endure at least a part of the tribulation period on earth.

Rapture Timeline Three—Jesus Will Come Before the Tribulation

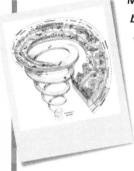

Many Christians believe that Jesus will return for his people *before* the tribulation period begins. Here's how future events will unfold in their opinion:

- Jesus will return in the air to take Christians out of the world.

- Shortly after the rapture, world events will take a dramatic turn for the worse. Corrupt world leaders will begin campaigns of war while God's judgments begin to fall.

- At the end of the seven-year tribulation, Jesus will return to earth in majesty and power.

- Jesus sweeps all remnants of human government from the earth and sets up a kingdom of peace.

This view is called the "pretribulation rapture" view. It simply means that the rapture will come *before* the tribulation period begins.

Arguments for the Defense

Proponents of the pretribulation rapture appeal to the following arguments to support their position:

1. The Bible promises that true followers of Jesus will be rescued from the time of God's judgment. A key verse is Revelation 3:10. Jesus was talking to the faithful believers in a early Christian community and he said: "Since you have kept my

God doesn't intend to punish us, but wants us to be saved by our Lord Jesus Christ.

1 Thessalonians 5:9 CEV

We should live soberly, righteously, and godly in the present age, looking for the blessed hope and glorious appearing of our great God and Savior Jesus Christ.

Titus 2:12–13 NKJV

command to endure patiently, I will also keep you from the hour of trial that is going to come upon the whole world to test those who live on the earth" (NIV). Jesus promises to keep believers from (literally, it could be translated *out of*) the future hour of trial that we call the tribulation.

2. The "church" or community of Christians is not pictured as being on earth during the tribulation. The apostle John gave his readers a lot of detail about the tribulation in Revelation chapters 6-19, but he talked about the church only in chapters 1-3. He pictured the church in heaven, not on earth, in chapters 4 and 5. (Most interpreters take the twenty-four elders seated around God's throne in Revelation 4:4 as a picture of Christians in heaven.) John did not refer to the church as being on earth again until the end of the tribulation, when "the bride" will return from heaven with Jesus (Revelation 19:7-8, 14).

3. Christians are told in the Bible to expect the rapture at any time. The New Testament writers seemed to anticipate the return of Jesus at any moment. This expectation suggests that the rapture will be the *first* event to occur. If the rapture comes at the end of the tribulation, it won't be a surprise to anyone.

Cross-Examination

The evidence for the pretribulation rapture sounds pretty convincing— but Christians who hold other views about the time of the rapture have raised some interesting questions.

1. The promises in the Bible about being delivered from the wrath and judgment of God refer to God's *eternal* wrath on human sin, not to the suffering we may experience on earth. In fact, the Bible specifically says that during this age Christians will suffer persecution from the world (John 16:33; Acts 14:22). Jesus also told two of the churches in Revelation 2 and 3 that they would experience "tribulation" and even "great tribulation" (Revelation 2:10, 22 NASB).

To expect God to rapture us out of the world before the tribulation period is to read too much into the biblical promises.

2. There are Scripture passages that seem to suggest that the New Testament writers did *not* expect Jesus to return at any moment. Jesus predicted, for example, that the city of Jerusalem would be destroyed (Matthew 24:1–2). That didn't happen until AD 70—many years after all of Paul's letters had been written and both Paul and Peter had been martyred.

3. While the book of Revelation does not use the word *church* to refer to believers on earth during the tribulation, it does talk about God's people or "saints" (a word frequently used of Christians in the New Testament). Revelation also describes a large multitude in heaven who had come out of the great tribulation (7:14)—clearly followers of Jesus who were martyred for their faith *during* the tribulation.

I looked, and behold, a door standing open in heaven . . . "Come up here, and I will show you what must take place after these things."

Revelation 4:1 NASB

The view that Jesus will return *for* his followers before the tribulation and *with* his church at the end of the tribulation is a widely held position among Christians. Most of the popular prophecy speakers and writers embrace this position—but, as you can see, it doesn't answer every question about future events, and there are other positions to consider.

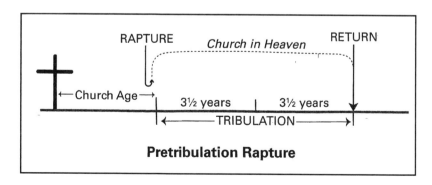

Pretribulation Rapture

Something to Ponder

Clouds are the mark of God's presence and power. Whenever God shows up in visible form in the Bible, he is usually surrounded by clouds of glory—and clouds are part of Jesus' return too. The apostle Paul says that at the rapture Christians will be caught up in the clouds (1 Thessalonians 4:17).

Check Your Understanding

- **Describe the pretribulational view of the rapture.**

Those who hold this view believe that Jesus will return to take his followers out of the world before the time of the tribulation begins.

- **Why is Revelation 3:10 such an important verse in this view?**

Jesus promised the faithful believers that he would keep them out of the hour of testing that was about to come on the whole world. This verse seems to indicate that true Christians will be taken out of the world before the tribulation begins.

- **Are there any indications in Scripture that the New Testament writers did *not* expect Jesus to return at any moment?**

Some passages of Scripture suggest that certain events will happen before Jesus' return. Jesus told Peter that Peter would die in his old age. Jesus also predicted that the city of Jerusalem would be destroyed, and that event didn't happen until AD 70.

Predictions That Went Very Wrong

Many people have tried to figure out the date of Jesus' return—and thousands of Christians have been swept into believing these date-setters. So far every one of them has been wrong! Even some future-tellers from other faiths have tried to predict the time of Jesus' return, but they have missed it too. The safest route is to just believe what Jesus said—no one has access to that information except God the Father, and he's not telling!

✳

A few examples will demonstrate how far off some date-setters have been:

- Christopher Columbus believed that he would fulfill prophecy through his explorations. He envisioned raising up a Christian army that would convert the world to Christianity. By his calculations the world would end in 1656.

The exact day and hour? No one knows that, not even heaven's angels, not even the Son. Only the Father.

Mark 13:32 MSG

It is not for you to know times or periods that the Father has set by His own authority.

Acts 1:7 HCSB

- On New Year's Eve, AD 999, Pope Sylvester II celebrated what he thought would be the last Mass of history. He based his view on Revelation 20:7–8, which he believed predicted a one-thousand-year church age until Jesus returned. Across Europe people had given away money and homes to the poor. Thousands of pilgrims flocked to Jerusalem, hoping to see Jesus descend from heaven. As midnight approached in Rome, Pope Sylvester raised his hands to heaven. The bells rang in the year 1000, but Jesus did not return.

- Edgar Whisenant predicted that Jesus would return in September 1988. Several million copies of his book *88 Reasons Why the Rapture*

Will Be in 1988 were sold. When September 1988 passed, Whisenant published a revised edition of his book and reset the date for October 3, 1989.

• Harold Camping went on his network of Christian radio stations in 1992 to announce that Jesus would return between September 15 and 27, 1994. Donations to his radio stations and newly formed church poured in. When September 27, 1994, passed, Camping simply said that he had miscalculated.

Something to Ponder

It is not only mainline Christians who have been wrong about Jesus' return and end-of-the-world scenarios.

> • Joseph Smith, the founder of Mormonism, wrote this prediction in his diary, dated April 6, 1843: "The Son of Man will not come in the heavens till I am 85 years old, 48 years hence, or about 1890."

• In 1990 Elizabeth Clare Prophet, a New Age visionary, issued a call to her followers to come to Montana in order to escape a nuclear war. Later the group leader claimed that her prayers had averted the disaster.

Digging Deeper

The fact that Christians don't know when Jesus will return should not be disappointing. Instead, the inability to figure it out should motivate followers of Jesus to be prepared for his coming at any time. What do you want to be doing when Jesus returns—faithfully following him or forgetfully pursuing your own agenda?

A Few Other Views About the Rapture

Most Bible teachers, prophecy speakers, and pastors hold one of the three views about the rapture that have been explored in previous chapters. But you don't have to search very long to find alternative views. Some of these views were once quite popular, but they fell out of favor for one reason or another. They have some biblical support but not enough to convince a majority or even a substantial number of Christians of their accuracy. They are interesting to think about, however—and even to toss into a debate with other Christians once in a while!

Here is just a sample of some of the views on the rapture that are floating around:

The Partial Rapture

This teaching says that Jesus will return for his people before the tribulation begins, but only *prepared* Christians will be taken out of the world. Unprepared Christians who are not fully committed to Jesus will remain on earth and will face the difficulties of the tribulation. The passage usually identified as supporting the position is Jesus' story about the ten virgins in Matthew 25:1-13. Five of the virgins were prepared for the bridegroom's arrival, and they were taken into the wedding celebration. The five virgins who were unprepared missed the bridegroom's coming and were left outside.

While they were gone to buy oil, the bridegroom came. Then [the virgins] who were ready went in with him to the marriage feast, and the door was locked.

Matthew 25:10 NLT

A few of you in Sardis have not dirtied your clothes with sin. You will walk with me in white clothes, because you are worthy.

Revelation 3:4 CEV

The Plural Rapture

A few people have tried to make a case for several points before and during the tribulation when Christians will be taken out of the world into heaven. They basically say that all the rapture views are correct, except that only some Christians are taken each time—the watching, faithful Christians are taken out before the tribulation, those who wise up and stay true to Jesus are taken out at midpoint, and others who find it difficult to remain loyal to Christ will be removed from earth only at the end of the tribulation.

If you do a search on the Internet or even at a local Christian bookstore, you can probably find one or two (or two thousand) alternate views on the rapture. The key to finding the correct view is to stay very close to the Bible's teaching.

Digging Deeper

Some churches talk very little about the rapture. They believe that everything will happen at the end in a "big bang"—Jesus will return; human beings will be resurrected and judged; eternity will begin. The rapture in their minds is not a single, distinguishable event but one aspect of the final climactic end-of-the-world event when Jesus returns. Christians who emphasize the rapture point to the fact that the biblical writers separate the rapture from the general event of Jesus' final return, so it must be a distinct event, not just one small part of a larger happening.

Something to Ponder

The apostle Paul closed his teaching on the rapture with this challenge: "Reassure one another with these words" (1 Thessalonians 4:18 MSG). The rapture is not designed to frighten you or to make you anxious; God wants it to encourage you. He wants it to strengthen your faith and your confidence in the future.

Terror at Every Turn—
The Tribulation

A time of great distress will come on the earth as God wraps up human history—a time of persecution and judgment like the world has never seen.

Contents

There will be strange signs in the sun. . . . And here on earth the nations will be in turmoil.

Luke 21:25 NLT

Seven Years of Horror—
Understanding the Tribulation

Movies have a way of scaring people to death! Sitting in a dark theater, you can almost believe the erupting volcanoes that swallow cities or the alien invasions or the nuclear missile attacks. What might surprise you is that someday some of the worst scenes you can imagine will actually break over the earth. The world is headed for disaster—not a disaster initiated by human beings, but a day of judgment from God. This period of distress and chaos is called the tribulation.

✳

A Specific Time

The word *tribulation* is used in the Bible in a general sense to mean "troubles" (1 Corinthians 7:28 NIV), "suffering" (Acts 7:11 NIV), "anguish" (John 16:21 NIV), and "hardships" (Acts 14:22 NIV). In a general sense, Christians will experience times of difficulty and hardship because of their faith or because they live in a world marked by sin and rebellion.

This is going to be trouble on a scale beyond what the world has ever seen, or will see again.

Matthew 24:21 MSG

But the word *tribulation* is also used to describe a specific time of distress that God will bring on the world. Jesus said that there would come a time of "great distress"— a time unequaled in world history and never to be equaled again (Matthew 24:21 NIV). The apostle John pictured men and women being martyred for their faith during

This is also what our dear friend Paul said when he wrote you with the wisdom that God had given him. . . . But part of what he says is hard to understand.

2 Peter 3:15–16 CEV

a time called "the great tribulation" (Revelation 7:14 NIV). Other biblical descriptions emphasize that God's judgment will be severe and intense. No one will escape.

A Biblical Teaching

The Bible talks about the tribulation in several places—in the Old Testament books of Daniel, Zechariah, and Zephaniah and in the New Testament Gospels and in Paul's letters. The book of Revelation devotes more than half its pages to a description of what the tribulation will be like. The apostle John (the human author of Revelation) didn't just read about those events; he saw them leap to life right in front of his eyes. John "saw" the future unfold, and then he wrote down what he saw so that his readers could "see" it too.

John didn't see the events in Revelation the way you would watch events on a television newsclip. John's visions were filled with symbols and images. Sometimes the images were identified, and sometimes they were not. For example, instead of seeing pictures of starving people lined up at a United Nation's feeding station, John saw a black horse ride out onto the world stage. The rider of the horse carried a pair of scales in his hand. A voice then announced that a small handful of wheat would cost a whole day's paycheck (Revelation 6:5-6). It's obviously a picture of famine sweeping the world, but John saw it in dramatic images.

A Unique Way of Communicating

God uses the images to make a powerful impression on John and on John's readers even today. It's one thing to read that an evil ruler will someday dominate the world; it's quite another thing to see an enormous Beast with seven heads rise out of the sea and conquer the world (Revelation 13:1-10). You might yawn through a recitation of simple words, but you won't be able to get an image like that out of your mind.

The images are not just John's unique way of jazzing up the story. Images represent real events or real people. The seven-headed Beast represents an evil ruler—the Antichrist. The black horse and its rider represent a real famine that will actually happen. Many of the symbols and images in Revelation can be identified by referring to hints in the text or by reading other passages of Scripture. A few of the images have baffled

Christian interpreters for centuries. If you find the book of Revelation difficult to understand in places, you join a long line of Christians who have scratched their heads over certain passages or specific images. No one can honestly claim to fully understand every detail. Some things will become clear only as the prophecy is fulfilled in the future.

The important thing to remember as you study Revelation (or biblical prophecy in general) is that John and the other writers were not just dreaming all of this up. God was giving them this information in its various forms, and God was guiding the prophets as they wrote the information down. The Bible contains an accurate record of what the prophets saw. The difficult part is trying to interpret that information accurately and consistently.

A Tribulation by Any Other Name

Some of the terms and phrases used in the Bible to refer to the tribulation:

Scripture	Term/Phrase*
Jeremiah 30:7	A time of trouble for Jacob
Zephaniah 1:14–16	The great day of the LORD A day of wrath A day of distress and anguish A day of trouble and ruin A day of darkness and gloom A day of clouds and blackness A day of trumpet and battle cry
Zephaniah 1:18	The day of the LORD's wrath The fire of [the LORD's] jealousy
Isaiah 34:8	A day of vengeance
Daniel 9:24–27	The final "seven"
Daniel 12:1	A time of distress such as has not happened from the beginning of nations until then
Joel 1:15	Destruction from the Almighty

Scripture	Term/Phrase*
Malachi 4:5	The great and dreadful day of the LORD
Matthew 24:8	Birth pains
1 Thessalonians 1:10	The coming wrath
Revelation 3:10	The hour of trial that is going to come upon the whole world
Revelation 6:17	The great day of [God's] wrath

* All phrases are from NIV.

Something to Ponder

 The proper response of every Christian to present troubles is hope, joy, and perseverance, knowing that God will ultimately conquer evil. The fact to remember is this: Although God's people will experience the wrath of evil powers in the world, they will never face God's wrath. "God chose to save us through our Lord Jesus Christ, not to pour out his anger on us" (1 Thessalonians 5:9 NLT).

The Preterist View—The Tribulation Is Past

Christians agree that the tribulation is real; what they don't agree on is *when* the tribulation will come and what *form* it will take. You may have been taught one particular view of the tribulation, and you may be convinced that your view is correct. The reality is that other Christians who are just as committed to Jesus and to the Bible as you are hold other views. When you have examined all the possibilities, you might find your own position strengthened—or changed.

✗

Some Christian believe that the predictions in the Bible about a time of great distress were fulfilled very soon after they were written. In their view, the tribulation is not some future period of time, but a series of events that happened in the past—about forty years after Jesus' death and resurrection.

In AD 70 the armies of the Roman Empire crushed a Jewish revolt in Judea, the land where Jesus had lived. The Romans devastated the land, killed hundreds of thousands of Jews, and leveled the city of Jerusalem. The temple where Jesus had taught (called the second temple, or Herod's temple) was burned to the ground. The massive stones of the city walls were pulled down. Jerusalem looked like a bombed-out, burned-out wasteland.

When you see Jerusalem surrounded by armies, then recognize that its desolation has come near.

Luke 21:20 HCSB

The Angel continued, "Don't seal the words of the prophecy of this book; don't put it away on the shelf. Time is just about up."

Revelation 22:10 MSG

This destruction was God's chastening of Israel for rejecting Jesus as her promised Messiah. Some people in Israel had believed in Jesus, but the nation as a whole, along with the religious leadership, had refused to accept him. The "tribulation" of the

Roman attack was God's way of showing everyone that the old way of worship and the old order of the Law had ended. God was now offering his grace and salvation through the new way of faith in Jesus alone.

In the Defense

Those who hold the view that the tribulation occurred in the past base their position on the following biblical teachings:

- Jesus, in a long sermon about the future, told his followers about tribulation events—wars and rumors of wars, famines, earthquakes, betrayals, and false Christs. Then Jesus added that "this age continues until all these things take place. Sky and earth will wear out; my words won't wear out" (Matthew 24:34-35 MSG). It seems that Jesus was telling his followers that the tribulation would occur in their lifetimes—and forty years later the Roman armies smashed Jerusalem.

- The "signs" that Jesus said would point to the approach of the tribulation were fulfilled by events in the first century. There was a protracted war between the Romans and the Jews (AD 67-70). A massive earthquake struck Jerusalem during the first year of the war with Rome.

- The "abomination" that Jesus said would appear in the temple (Matthew 24:15 NIV) referred to the Roman insignia carried by the troops. These were adorned with religious images that God specifically prohibited in Israel's worship.

- Those who hold the view that the tribulation is past assert that the apostle John received the visions of the book of Revelation during the reign of the Roman emperor Nero (AD 54-68) a few years *before* the Roman war in Judea.

- Chapters 4-19 of Revelation describe the tribulation in symbolic terms, but it was all fulfilled in AD 70. The "coming" of the Son of Man (Matthew 24:30) that Jesus talked about was *not* the visible return of Jesus but his "coming" in judgment against Israel.

On the Other Hand

Christians who hold differing views of the time of the tribulation have raised some interesting questions about the "AD 70 tribulation" position.

- The Old Testament prophets, Jesus, and the book of Revelation all make it clear that the tribulation will end with the *rescue* of Israel and the *destruction* of the enemy armies. The exact reverse happened in AD 70—Israel was crushed and the Roman armies were victorious.

- The view that the prophecies about the tribulation were fulfilled in Judea in AD 70 hardly fits with the global language used in the book of Revelation to describe the catastrophic judgments of God. The events in one tiny province of the Roman Empire just don't fit.

Jerusalem, Jerusalem! Your people have killed the prophets and have stoned the messengers who were sent to you. . . . And now your temple will be deserted.

Matthew 23:37–38 CEV

- Jesus' statement that "this generation will certainly not pass away" (Matthew 24:34 NIV) does not have to be restricted to the generation to which Jesus was talking. He could mean that the generation alive when the final events *begin* to happen will not pass away until it has all been fulfilled.

Digging Deeper

The position that the tribulation happened in the past is called the *preterist* view. The term comes from the Latin word *praeteritus*, which means "gone by" or "past." Some prominent Christian leaders who have held this view are Origen (185–254), John Calvin (1509–1564), and Matthew Henry (1662–1714). The main contemporary defenders of the "tribulation is past" view are R. C.

Sproul, Kenneth Gentry, Gary DeMar, and David Chilton. The preterist view is usually held by those who are also *amillennial* or *postmillennial* in their view of God's kingdom.

What Others Say

I hold that the Tribulation occurred in our distant past in the first century. . . . I hold that the Tribulation closes out the Jewish-based, old covenant order, and establishes the new covenant (Christian) order. . . . Preterism holds that the Tribulation prophecies occur in the first century, thus in our past.

Kenneth L. Gentry Jr.

Something to Ponder

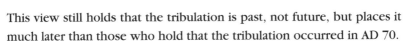

Some preterist interpreters believe that the book of Revelation predicts the fall of the Roman Empire ("Babylon the Great") in AD 476. God would judge the entire Roman system for persecuting Christians who had refused to worship the emperor as a divine being. The warning of Revelation to Christians is not to compromise with this idolatrous system. God comforts them with the promise that he will eventually judge their enemies.

This view still holds that the tribulation is past, not future, but places it much later than those who hold that the tribulation occurred in AD 70.

The Idealist View—The Tribulation Is Timeless

Another approach to understanding the tribulation is called the *idealist* view. According to this perspective, the predictions in the Bible about the tribulation represent the ongoing conflict between good and evil in the world. These conflicts exist in every period of history. The Christians who hold this view of the tribulation argue that the symbols used in prophecy do not represent any single event in the past or in the future but themes and trends in any age. The "Beast," for example, in Revelation 13 is not a single oppressive ruler but a symbol of oppressive political power at any time in history.

Christians who hold to an idealist position defend their view by appealing more to general biblical themes than to specific statements of Scripture.

Positive Points

• The idealist approach allows prophecy to apply directly and powerfully to each generation of readers. If the biblical descriptions of the tribulation point readers to timeless principles at work in every generation, then each generation of Christians can apply those principles to what they are experiencing today.

• Reading biblical prophecy as a picture of the struggle in every age between good and evil prompts Christians to courageous living and faithful endurance, no matter how oppressive the circumstances.

• John, the author of Revelation, even said that some Christians in his day were in tribulation or

I, John, your brother and fellow partaker in the tribulation and kingdom and perseverance which are in Jesus . . .

Revelation 1:9 NASB

In the world you will have tribulation; but be of good cheer, I have overcome the world.

John 16:33 NKJV

distress as he wrote (Revelation 2:9-10, 22)—which shows that John did not have one specific time period in mind for these prophecies but was focused instead on timeless principles. Revelation reminds Christians in every age that God still rules from his throne, even over a world in chaos.

Quality Questions

Every Christian would agree that Revelation is a reminder that God rules, but many would challenge the idealist interpretation.

- Why does God give such detailed information about the tribulation if he did not intend for Christians to think that actual historical events were being described?

- Since almost all the prophecies about Jesus' first coming were fulfilled literally, isn't it logical to conclude that the prophecies surrounding his second coming will also be fulfilled literally?

Something to Ponder

Those who believe that the tribulation is already past put the emphasis on the original readers of the book of Revelation and the political circumstances of the first century. Those who believe that the tribulation is a timeless parable emphasize the relevance of the book for present-day readers. Those who believe that the tribulation is still future emphasize the value of knowing in advance God's plan for human history.

What Others Say

We must resist the temptation to link each trumpet [referring to the trumpet judgments recorded in Revelation 8-9] with a particular date or person in history. The trumpets indicate a series of happenings or calamities that will occur again and again throughout the earthly existence of the church.

Sam Hamstra

The Futurist View—The Tribulation Is Coming

The third view of where the tribulation fits into God's plan for human history is called the *futurist* view. Christians who hold this view believe that the Bible's predictions about the tribulation will be fulfilled in a time of intense judgment from God in the future.

This future seven-year period will begin when a prominent world leader signs a peace treaty with Israel. The tribulation will end when Jesus returns from heaven in power and splendor to destroy his enemies and to rescue his people.

An Outline of the Tribulation

Futurists see the tribulation unfolding like this:

- During the first three and a half years of the tribulation, war, famine, and disaster will sweep over the world in waves. Powerful forces of evil will gain control over human society.
- In the middle of the tribulation, the world leader who had made peace with Israel will invade that nation and proclaim himself to be God in the rebuilt temple in Jerusalem. That act will reveal the leader to be the Antichrist.
- Wave after wave of judgment will crash down on the world during the second half of the tribulation. Finally the Antichrist will gather the armies of the world around Jerusalem with the intention of destroying the Jews. Jesus will return at the moment things seem most desperate.

> I saw the beast and the kings of the world and their armies gathered together to fight against the one sitting on the horse.
>
> Revelation 19:19 NLT
>
> Then there will be a time of anguish greater than any since nations first came into existence.
>
> Daniel 12:1 NLT

Speaking for the Defense

Those who are convinced that the tribulation is a future event base their view on the following biblical information:

• This is the only view that takes a consistently literal approach to how the words of biblical prophecy are understood. Prophecy does include symbols and symbolic language, but futurists believe that the symbols represent actual events and people.

• The magnitude of the prophecies about the future (the sun is darkened; one-third of the world's fresh water is polluted) suggests that these events have not yet occurred in history. Nothing in the destruction of Jerusalem in AD 70 or in any period of time since then corresponds to the range or severity of these biblical predictions.

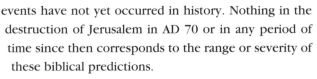

• God did not *replace* the people of Israel in his program or *transfer* the Old Testament promises from Israel to the Christian church. The earthly kingdom promised in the Old Testament was *postponed* because of Israel's rejection of Jesus as the Messiah. God, however, has not forgotten these promises.

• According to Jesus (in Matthew 24) and the book of Revelation, the tribulation ends with the people of Israel (Jews living in the land of Israel) coming to faith in Jesus and being rescued from the oppression of the Antichrist. In AD 70 the Jews in Jerusalem were killed or driven out of the city. The destruction of Jerusalem in the first century could not have been the tribulation predicted in the Bible.

• The book of Revelation was written too late for its prophecies to be fulfilled in AD 70. The abundance of evidence from the early church places the date of the composition of Revelation *after* AD 70—most likely somewhere between AD 85 and 95!

Cross-Examination

Those Christians who believe that the tribulation is past or that the tribulation principles are at work in every generation have not let futurists off the hook when it comes to tough challenges.

- What about the repeated statements of the biblical writers that these events of the tribulation would "soon" take place or that "the time is near"? Do futurists take these words literally too?

- Futurists have gone overboard on their "literal" interpretation and have missed the point. Some prophecy pundits have tried to find end-times fulfillment in every newspaper headline. The futurists have pressed the interpretation of prophecy too far. God wanted his people to get the big picture, not microanalyze the details.

> The sun will become dark, and the moon will no longer shine. The stars will fall, and the powers in the sky will be shaken.
>
> Matthew 24:29 CEV

- The view that the tribulation is future totally removes the relevance of the book of Revelation for John's original readers—and even for readers today. How can predictions about events far in the future bring comfort to people who are suffering persecution right now?

- The predictions of judgment in Revelation are not global or worldwide in scope. Most of the references to "the earth" should instead be translated "the land," meaning the land of Judea, where most of the Jews lived in the first century. They experienced the judgment of the tribulation. It is not for some future generation at all.

What Others Say

I do not believe the Bible teaches that the Tribulation is in any way past. Instead, Scripture tells us that it is a *future* event that could commence very soon.

Thomas Ice

Few events can claim equal significance as far as Bible prophecy is concerned as that of the return of Israel to their land. It constitutes a preparation for the end of the age.

John Walvoord

Digging Deeper

Futurist interpreters of the book of Revelation see an outline of the book's contents in Revelation 1:19: "Write, therefore, what you have seen [Revelation 1], what is now [Revelation 2-3] and what will take place later [Revelation 4-22]" (NIV).

Many influential leaders in the early church were basically futurist in this view of biblical prophecy—Justin Martyr, Irenaeus, Hippolytus. The view faded, however, with the rise of a more allegorical, spiritual method of interpretation under Augustine in the fifth century. After the Protestant Reformation and the revivals of the nineteenth century, the futurist view began to make a comeback.

Something to Ponder

Many students of prophecy see an Islamic connection to biblical prophecy in Ezekiel 38. They believe that "Gog" represents the modern nation of Russia and that all of Gog's allies are Islamic countries. They conclude that Ezekiel 38 describes a future invasion of Israel by Russia and a group of what are today Islamic nations—  Turkey, Sudan, Libya, and Iran. The religion of Islam, of course, came into existence centuries after the Bible was written, so no direct references to Islam are found in Scripture.

Comparing the Different Tribulation Viewpoints

Each of the three views on how the tribulation should be interpreted is held by sincere Christians who claim that they understand the Bible as God intended it to be understood. No one doubts their commitment to Jesus or their sincerity in defending their particular view. But which view is the right one? Is it possible that each view tells part of the story—that each view emphasizes one aspect of the truth, but not the whole truth?

Those Christians who believe that the tribulation happened in the first century when Jerusalem was destroyed by the Roman army emphasize God's powerful works of judgment in the past and the impact of prophecy on the original readers. But does the past tell the whole story? Maybe the past "distress" was a *pre-fillment* of the Bible's predictions about the tribulation, and the *full-fillment* is yet to come in the future. God's work of judgment isn't finished yet. What Israel experienced in part in AD 70 will be experienced by the whole world in the future time of distress.

> You will be brought before kings and rulers for My name's sake. But it will turn out for you as an occasion for testimony.
>
> Luke 21:12–13 NKJV
>
> I have appeared to you to appoint you as my servant and witness. You are to tell the world what you have seen and what I will show you in the future.
>
> Acts 26:16 NLT

While the events of the past and the predictions for the future are interesting to study, maybe Christians today need to let prophecy speak more directly to their lives in the modern world, as the idealist suggests. It's one thing to debate how anyone will survive the cruelty of the Antichrist; it's something else to survive persecution and slavery in Sudan today or to stand for the faith against the official opposition of the North Korean government. It's too easy for Christians in Western democracies to relegate the book of Revelation to some future day and to forget the brothers and sisters in Christ who may be experiencing the equivalent of the tribulation right now. And one more thing—shouldn't the Bible's predictions about future suffering prompt courageous living today—and a sense of urgency to spread the message of God's grace and deliverance from the wrath to come?

Digging Deeper

Here's how the three tribulation views interpret the appearance of the "Beast" in Revelation 13:

- *Tribulation Is Past View.* The Roman emperor Nero rose up to persecute Christians and ordered the initial attack on Jerusalem.

- *Tribulation Is Timeless View.* Satan works through evil governments to oppress God's people in every age.

- *Tribulation Is Future View.* An evil leader, the Antichrist, will emerge during the tribulation and will seek to dominate the world.

Points to Remember

- The tribulation is a time of God's judgment on a world that has rejected him.

- Christians have proposed several ways to understand how the tribulation fits into God's plan.

- The future tribulation will end with the visible return of Jesus to earth.

What Daniel Predicted About the Tribulation

Six hundred years before Jesus was born, a young boy was taken from his home in Jerusalem and brought to Babylon, the capital of a great empire. Eventually, the boy became a prophet of God, a spokesman for the Lord to the political movers and shakers of his day. One day, as Daniel was reading the writings of another prophet, Jeremiah, he realized that God had predicted the release of the people of Israel at the end of seventy years of captivity. Daniel thought the promised kingdom on earth would begin at that point. But God sent an angel to give him another message.

The Prophecy

The angel Gabriel told Daniel that Israel would have to wait longer than seventy years for the kingdom. They would have to pass through "seventy 'sevens'" (most often understood as seventy times seven years, seventy "weeks" of years, or 490 years) before the kingdom would begin. (The prophecy is in Daniel 9:24-27.)

The event that would start the clock ticking on the 490 years was a decree to rebuild and restore the city of Jerusalem. The "seventy 'sevens'" are then divided into three sections.

> Seventy sevens are set for your people and for your holy city to throttle rebellion, stop sin, wipe out crime, set things right forever.
>
> Daniel 9:24 MSG
>
> When you see the abomination that causes desolation, spoken of by the prophet Daniel, standing in the holy place (let the reader understand) . . .
>
> Matthew 24:15 HCSB

Division 1—Seven "Sevens"
(49 Years)

Most biblical scholars believe the decree Gabriel referred to was issued by King Artaxerxes in 445 BC. It allowed Nehemiah to rebuild Jerusalem and began the countdown of 490 years.

Division 2—Sixty-two "Sevens" (434 Years)

The second division of years in God's prophecy to Daniel spanned 434 years. The 49 years of division 1 and the 434 years of division 2 brought the people of Judah to the time of Jesus' public ministry. God adds this fact in Daniel 9:26: "After the sixty-two 'sevens,' the Anointed One [Messiah] will be cut off and will have nothing" (NIV).

God told his people exactly when the Messiah would come—and he told them more than five hundred years before Jesus' birth. God also implied that there would be an interval of time between the second division of the prophecy (sixty-two weeks) and the third division (the seventieth week). The Messiah would be cut off, that is, violently killed, *after* the first 483 years. God also said that Jerusalem would be destroyed—an event that happened forty years after Jesus was crucified—another "gap" of time between division 2 and division 3.

Division 3—The Final "Week" of Years (Seven Years)

Christians have different views about where the seventieth "week" fits into God's program. Some say that after Jesus died and rose again, the kingdom of God was established through the Christian church, the new Israel.

Other Christians believe that the interval before the final period of seven years is still continuing today. National Israel rejected Jesus as the Messiah. As a result, the promised kingdom was *postponed*, not transferred to the church. The church age has intervened for two thousand years, but when the church (the true followers of Jesus) is taken out of the world at the rapture, the clock will start ticking again on the final seven years.

The "seventieth week" of Daniel will be the seven years of the tribulation. God will focus again on national Israel. At the end of the seven years, Jesus will return in glory and will set up his kingdom on earth.

The Antichrist

The prophecy in Daniel even talked about tribulation events. God said that a ruler will make a covenant with many for one "seven,"—one period of seven years, the last one. But in the middle of that "seven," he will put an end to Israel's sacrifices and will set up an abomination (Daniel 9:27). These statements are picked up by Jesus in the New Testament as references to the Antichrist's intrusion into the temple and the setting up of an image of himself to be worshiped (Matthew 24:15–21).

> The woman ran into the desert to a place that God had prepared for her. There she would be taken care of for one thousand two hundred sixty days.
>
> Revelation 12:6 CEV

Daniel's framework of seven years also fits the time references in the book of Revelation. Various phrases mark out the two halves of the tribulation as three and a half years each. The apostle John said that the time the Gentiles trample on the city of Jerusalem and defile the temple, for example, would be forty-two months (Revelation 11:2; see also Revelation 11:3; 12:6; 12:14; and 13:5).

So when you hear a prophecy preacher refer to "Daniel's seventieth week," you will know that he's talking about the future seven years of the tribulation. The first sixty-nine "weeks" of years are already ancient history; the final "week" of years is yet to come.

Digging Deeper

Predicted events from Daniel 9:24–27 that have already happened:

- A decree to rebuild Jerusalem was issued (Nehemiah 2:7–8).

- The people of Israel were released from captivity (Ezra 1:1–5).

- The temple was rebuilt (Ezra 6:15-17).

- The city walls were rebuilt (Nehemiah 6:15-16).

- 483 years passed between the decree to rebuild the city and the coming of the Messiah.

- The Messiah came to Israel and was violently killed (Matthew 27:35).

- Jerusalem was destroyed in AD 70.

- The temple was destroyed and has not been rebuilt.

Myth Buster

Because the prophecies in the book of Daniel are so detailed and so accurate, some scholars have concluded that the book was written *after* all the events had taken place. In this view "Daniel" never existed; he was just created by a later writer as a vehicle to tell the story. Other scholars believe the evidence points to a very real Daniel who lived during the time of Babylon's empire. The accuracy of the predictions in Daniel's book comes from the ability of God to know future events and to reveal those events to his prophets.

Something to Ponder

If God offered to tell you the future of your family or your nation over the next four hundred years, would you want to hear it or not? Usually God just gives his people the light they need for the next step, not the next mile or the next week.

144,000 Jewish Believers

Through the testimony of two witnesses in Israel, 144,000 Jewish people will believe in Jesus as their Messiah and will be sealed with God's protection (Revelation 7:1–8; 14:1–5). These messianic Jews will be scattered throughout the world during the tribulation. They will preach the message of Jesus' soon return to earth in power and majesty—and thousands of people will receive their message! One of the greatest revivals in history will sweep the world during the tribulation. Many of those who believe in Jesus, however, will be martyred for their allegiance to Christ.

In the middle of judgments and the rise of evil rulers, John, the writer of Revelation, gave his readers glimpses of God's redemptive work. The Bible reveals the following information about a group of 144,000 who faithfully follow Jesus during the tribulation:

• They are sealed with the seal of the living God (Revelation 7:2).

• They are servants of God (Revelation 7:3).

• They are from all the tribes of Israel (Revelation 7:4).

• They stand on Mount Zion with the Lamb (Revelation 14:1).

• They have the Lamb's name and the Father's name on their foreheads (Revelation 14:1).

• They sing a new song before God's throne (Revelation 14:3).

• They do not defile themselves (Revelation 14:4).

> Don't harm the earth or the sea or the trees until we seal the slaves of our God on their foreheads.
>
> Revelation 7:3 HCSB

> This great choir sang a wonderful new song. . . . No one could learn this song except the 144,000 who had been redeemed from the earth.
>
> Revelation 14:3 NLT

- They follow the Lamb wherever he goes (Revelation 14:4).

- No lie is found in their words, and they are blameless (Revelation 14:5).

These characteristics have been interpreted in two ways:

- Some take the 144,000 as a literal number of Jews who become Christians during the tribulation and preach the message of Jesus through the world. John made it clear that these were from the tribes of Israel, that is, Jews (Revelation 7:4).

- A second view sees the 144,000 as representative of all true followers of Jesus during the tribulation. Just as the followers of the Antichrist have the mark of the Beast on their foreheads, the followers of Christ are sealed with the seal of God.

Something to Ponder

The Bible's image of 144,000 servants of God has stirred controversy for nearly two thousand years. Charles Russell, one of the founders of the Jehovah's Witnesses, claimed that God was choosing 144,000 "spiritual Israelites" to make up his true church. These king-priests would reign with Christ in the kingdom. When Russell's followers numbered *more* than 144,000, he added a second class of heavenly servants—the "great company" or "other sheep."

What Others Say

It is very clear, therefore, that the sealed multitude of Revelation 7 symbolizes the entire Church.

William Hendriksen

This is not the entirety of the faithful remnant of Israel, but a group of them charged with a special responsibility of witnessing for Christ during the world's darkest hour.

Robert Thomas

Two Powerful Evangelists—The Two Witnesses

As the visions of the book of Revelation unfolded, John heard about two witnesses who would speak with God's authority for 1,260 days (about three and a half years). These two witnesses will be given powers that are reminders of the powers that were given to some Old Testament prophets. In fact, it may be that a couple of those prophets return to earth! The two witnesses will preach to the people of Israel and will prepare them for the betrayal of the world ruler they have come to trust for their nation's security.

The first issue that readers of Revelation 11 have to deal with is who are the two witnesses? The apostle John said that they will have the power to close the sky so that it won't rain and the power to turn water into blood and the power to produce fire to consume their enemies (Revelation 11:5-6). In the Old Testament, Elijah called down fire (2 Kings 1:10, 12) and stopped the rain in Israel (1 Kings 17:1). Moses turned water into blood when the pharaoh refused to release the people of Israel (Exodus 7:17-21). Some students of prophecy think God will bring these same two prophets back to earth during the future tribulation. Others believe that the two witnesses will have powers *similar* to those of Elijah and Moses, but they will be two new prophets sent from God.

> My two witnesses will wear sackcloth, while I let them preach for one thousand two hundred sixty days.
>
> Revelation 11:3 CEV

> Elijah, for instance, human just like us, prayed hard that it wouldn't rain, and it didn't—not a drop for three and a half years.
>
> James 5:17 MSG

The two witnesses will preach in Israel during the first three and a half years of the tribulation. It is most likely through their testimony that the 144,000 servants of God will be converted and equipped to preach the message of Jesus to the whole world. When the Antichrist invades Israel, however, in the middle of the tribulation, one of his first priorities will be to silence these witnesses. They will be murdered, and their bodies will lie in the streets of Jerusalem for three and a half days. Then, by the power of God, the witnesses will be raised back to life and taken into heaven in a cloud (Revelation 11:3–13).

Something to Ponder

Another suggestion for the identities of these two witnesses is Elijah and Enoch. Enoch was taken directly to heaven without dying (Genesis 5:24; Hebrews 11:5). The prophet Elijah was also taken directly to heaven in a fiery chariot (2 Kings 2:11–12). Since these two men did not die (so the argument goes), they may be the ones who return to earth as God's witnesses and suffer death in the tribulation.

Digging Deeper

The two witnesses emphasize the role of courageous testimony. They are empowered by God; they confront a wicked world; they are temporarily conquered; but, in the end, they overcome by God's power and their own faithfulness. Ultimately, they are ushered into the safety of God's presence.

Seals, Trumpets, and Bowls

Three waves of judgments will sweep through the earth during the tribulation. The first wave will come early in the tribulation as Jesus breaks seven wax seals on a scroll in heaven (Revelation 5–8). The second wave will come toward the middle of the tribulation as seven angels in heaven blow seven trumpets (Revelation 8–9). The final wave will come near the end of the tribulation as seven angels pour bowls (or vials) of judgment on the earth from heaven (Revelation 16).

Seal Judgments

In his vision of heaven, the apostle John saw Jesus take a scroll from God the Father and begin to break the seals. As each seal was broken, John saw a new image leap to life from the scroll.

- The first seal: A conqueror on a white horse—the emergence of the Antichrist on the world scene (Revelation 6:1-2).

- The second seal: A rider on a red horse—wars and threats of wars will shake human society (Revelation 6:3-4).

> Judah, the heir to David's throne, has won the victory. He is worthy to open the scroll and its seven seals.
>
> Revelation 5:5 NLT

- The third seal: A rider on a black horse—wars and upheavals will produce famines in some parts of the world (Revelation 6:5-6).

> The seventh angel sounded. . . . "The kingdoms of this world have become the kingdoms of our Lord and of His Christ!"
>
> Revelation 11:15 NKJV

- The fourth seal: A rider on a pale horse—death will claim one-fourth of the earth's population (Revelation 6:7-8).

- The fifth seal: Those martyred for their loyalty to Jesus will cry out for justice (Revelation 6:9-11).

- The sixth seal: A great earthquake and cosmic disturbances (Revelation 6:12–17).

- The seventh seal: Silence in heaven as seven angels with trumpets prepare for the next wave of judgments (Revelation 8:1–2).

The seal judgments will be dreadful but not as severe as later judgments. Each of these catastrophes can be attributed to human initiative or to natural disasters. Later judgments will be clearly the intervention of God.

Trumpet Judgments

At the midpoint of the seven years of distress, seven trumpet judgments will fall on humankind.

- The first trumpet: Hail and fire will destroy one-third of the earth's vegetation (Revelation 8:7).

- The second trumpet: A huge burning mountain will be thrown into the sea; one-third of the sea life will die (Revelation 8:8–9).

- The third trumpet: A great star (meteor?) will fall from heaven and pollute the fresh water (Revelation 8:10–11).

- The fourth trumpet: The sun, moon, and stars will be diminished by one-third (Revelation 8:12–13).

- The fifth trumpet: An angel will open a stronghold where demonic forces have been confined (Revelation 9:1–12).

- The sixth trumpet: Massive armies from the East will move toward Israel, spreading destruction in their path (Revelation 9:13–21).

- The seventh trumpet: Those in heaven will rejoice over God's ultimate triumph (Revelation 11:15–19).

The trumpet judgments are more intense and severe than the seal judgments. Many of them parallel the plagues that God brought on Egypt when the pharaoh refused to release Israel from slavery. The figure of "a third" used in each of the first four trumpet judgments reveals that God's judgments are partial, but not yet final. The last three trumpet judgments are described as "woes" (Revelation 8:13) and will be directed at the inhabitants of the earth, not at the natural world as the first four trumpet judgments were.

Bowl Judgments

As the tribulation comes to an end, seven angels will appear in heaven, carrying bowls that represent God's wrath.

Yes, Lord God, the Almighty, true and righteous are Your judgments.

Revelation 16:7 HCSB

• The first bowl: Painful sores will fall on all who have the Antichrist's mark (Revelation 16:2).

• The second bowl: The oceans will turn to blood and all sea life will die (Revelation 16:3).

• The third bowl: Fresh water will turn to blood (Revelation 16:4-7).

• The fourth bowl: The sun will scorch human beings with intense heat (Revelation 16:8-9).

• The fifth bowl: Agonizing darkness will fall over the Antichrist's realm (Revelation 16:10-11).

• The sixth bowl: The Euphrates River will dry up to prepare the way for armies from the East (Revelation 16:12).

• The seventh bowl: A devastating earthquake will rock the earth, and huge hailstones will fall from the sky (Revelation 16:17-21).

The seventh bowl judgment will bring history to a close. The voice from the heavenly temple and throne will proclaim: "It is done"—that is, it is over; man's day has come to an end.

Further Insight

The first four seal judgments (Revelation 6:1-8) are better known as the "four horsemen of the Apocalypse." The Lamb opened each seal in John's vision and John then saw a horse of a particular color and a rider who executes judgment. These four riders and their horses are often used in literature or art as symbols of doom or of the end of the world. It's possible to see all four of these judgments at work in today's world, but they will mark the entire seven years of the tribulation.

Something to Ponder

One unusual feature of the bowl judgments appears just before the seventh bowl is poured out. John recorded the warning of Jesus to his followers to stay awake and alert because his coming would be unexpected, like a thief in the night (Revelation 16:15). The one who stays awake and is clothed will be blessed rather than exposed to shame and rebuke. Jesus' warning points to the central message of biblical prophecy—in light of the approaching conflict, believers should remain faithful and loyal to Jesus. No compromise!

Final Thoughts

When the sixth seal on the heavenly scroll is opened, a question is asked: "Who can stand?" It means who can survive or endure the coming wrath of God? The seventh chapter of Revelation provides the answer: Only the servants of God can survive—they will experience God's deliverance rather than his wrath.

The Antichrist and a Satanic Trinity

An evil world ruler will emerge on the scene in the tribulation, and he will seek to conquer the world and destroy God's people. An evil "trinity" will seek to set up a kingdom on earth to rival God's kingdom in heaven—and they will fail disastrously!

Contents

The Lord Jesus will destroy him with the breath of His mouth and will bring him to nothing with the brightness of His coming.

2 Thessalonians 2:8 HCSB

Is the Antichrist a Person or a Power?

Some pretty nasty rulers have walked across the world stage in the past two thousand years—men and women who have risen to power and left a legacy of oppression, war, and murder. As incredibly evil as these people of the past have been, the worst is yet to come. The Bible predicts the rise of a future ruler who will set out to conquer the world—and who will almost succeed. He will demand not simply loyalty from his subjects but adoration and worship. Those who resist or refuse will be crushed. This future ruler is called the Beast, or the Antichrist.

Not all Christians view this future ruler as an actual person. Some believe that the Beast of Revelation is a symbol of evil and of oppressive governments. The Beast (according to this view) is not a literal person but the embodiment of humanity's rebellion against God in every age. They point to passages in the Bible where the term *antichrist* does not mean an individual person but a willful spirit of disobedience to God.

Here's one example: "Every spirit that does not acknowledge Jesus is not from God. This is the spirit of the antichrist, which you have heard is coming and even now is already in the world" (1 John 4:3 NIV). See also 1 John 2:18, 22; 2 John 7.

I saw a Beast rising from the sea. . . . It held absolute sway over all tribes and peoples, tongues and races.

Revelation 13:1, 7 MSG

Children, it is the last hour; and just as you heard that antichrist is coming, even now many antichrists have appeared; from this we know that it is the last hour.

1 John 2:18 NASB

As you read that verse, it sounds as though the Antichrist is not some future ruler but a present, pervading spirit in human culture. At the same time, John was not denying the appearance of a future evil ruler. He said in 1 John 2:18 (NIV): "The antichrist *is* coming" (emphasis added). The evil tendencies that will find fulfillment in the future Antichrist are already alive and active in the world today. The *spirit* of opposition to God is already at work; the *fulfillment* of that spirit will be accomplished in one person who rises to world power and sets himself against God.

Digging Deeper

 Some interpreters of the book of Revelation believe that John was writing about his own time, not a future time. John was producing a sketch of events going on around him, but in a prophetic "code" that only other Christians would understand. According to this view, when John saw a Beast come out of the sea in his vision, John was not describing some future world ruler but the "Beastly" Roman emperor of his own day.

Check Your Understanding

- **Who is the Antichrist in biblical prophecy?**

Most students of prophecy believe that the Antichrist is a future world ruler who will rise to power during the tribulation and who will persecute the followers of Jesus.

- **In what ways does the *spirit* of antichrist reveal itself?**

The spirit of antichrist is active in every age. It is seen most directly in the persecution of Christians and the oppression of the church by evil rulers and governments. The spirit also reveals itself in humanity's general attitude of rebellion against God and the refusal of many human beings to submit to God's commands.

Biblical Names for the Antichrist

The Bible uses several names and descriptive titles for the Antichrist. Each name is designed to give you some insight into the Antichrist's character or actions. In fact, a person's *name* in biblical culture was chosen to help other people understand something about their true nature. The names of God, for example, are descriptions of who God really is and how God works. The same principle applies to the names and titles of the Antichrist.

It's helpful to examine the names of the Antichrist in the reverse order in which they appear in the Bible. The later names are clearer and more descriptive.

• *The Beast*—Revelation 13:1. The favorite name for the Antichrist in the book of Revelation is "the Beast." The apostle John saw a grotesque Beast-like creature arise from the "sea" of the nations. The Antichrist will not, of course, be a grotesque being; he will be winsome and well-loved. But in his inner nature, the Antichrist will be like a ferocious wild animal.

> I am about to raise up a shepherd in the land who will not care for those who are going astray, and he will not seek the lost or heal the broken.
>
> Zechariah 11:15 HCSB

> The Beast I saw looked like a leopard with bear paws and a lion's mouth. The Dragon turned over its power to it, its throne and great authority.
>
> Revelation 13:2 MSG

• *The Antichrist*—1 John 2:18. The term *Antichrist* carries the meaning of a false Christ and of standing against Christ.

• *The Lawless One* or *The Man of Lawlessness*—2 Thessalonians 2:3, 8. The Antichrist will be a tyrant of a ruler and will demand unwavering obedience, but he will consider himself above any rule of law.

- *The Foolish* (or *Worthless*) *Shepherd*—Zechariah 11:15-17. This title describes the Antichrist's relationship with the people of Israel. In contrast to Israel's *true* Shepherd (the Lord), the Antichrist will be a wicked and untrustworthy leader.

- *The King*—Daniel 11:36.

- *The Ruler Who Will Come*—Daniel 9:26. This title ties the Antichrist with a revived Roman Empire. The Romans would execute the *true* Christ; the Antichrist will arise from the remnants of the same political entity.

- *A Little Horn*—Daniel 7:8. In a vision of another Beast, Daniel saw the Antichrist arise as an insignificant ruler (a small horn) who eventually will gain great power.

Digging Deeper

The Beast that John saw looked like a leopard (swift, deadly) but also had some features like a bear (powerful) and a lion (terrifying). The Antichrist, of course, will not literally have animal features, but the symbols represent aspects of his character as well as his effect on people around him. The Old Testament prophet Daniel had used the same animals to picture the "Beastly" nature of other world empires, empires that existed long ago. The future Beast will combine the worst of the old and the worst of the new.

Essential Passages on an Evil Ruler

Daniel 11:36–12:1	2 Thessalonians 2:1–10	Revelation 13:1–9
The evil character	The man of lawlessness of the Antichrist.	The Beast rises to political power.
His invasion of Israel	He sets himself up as god.	He persecutes God's people.

Who Is the Beast?—Differing Perspectives

Christians have taken different approaches to the understanding of biblical prophecy and to the interpretation of the book of Revelation. The overall perspective you take will determine the person or entity that you determine to be the Antichrist. You won't agree with all the positions explained below—in fact, you *can't* agree with all of them—but it is interesting to step back and get a differing viewpoint.

Happened in the Past

The view that the book of Revelation was written to describe events that happened in the first century, not in some future time, is called the *preterist* view. (The word *preterist* means "past.") Under this interpretive approach, the horrible "Beast" of Revelation 13 is the Roman Empire (or a Roman emperor) that is bent on crushing the Christian church. John wrote down his visions as an encouragement to Christians undergoing persecution and as a veiled protest against the evils of Roman authority.

Many deceivers have gone out into the world. They deny that Jesus Christ came in a real body. Such a person is a deceiver and an antichrist.

2 John 7 NLT

The Antichrist *is* coming.

1 John 2:18 NKJV, emphasis added

Happens in Every Age

According to the *idealist* view, Revelation describes the ongoing conflict between good and evil throughout every age. You could find a Beast-like ruler somewhere in the world today who is persecuting Christians and standing defiantly against God. According to this view, the Beast in Revelation 13 represents state authority that rises up at any time or in any place in opposition to the church. Such "Antichrists" have appeared several times in history.

Yet to Happen

The *futurist* view holds that all of John's visions from Revelation 4:1 through the end of the book are yet to be fulfilled. John was clearly told in Revelation 4:1 that he would be shown events that "must take place *after this*" (NKJV, emphasis added)—that is, after John's own lifetime. According to this approach, the Beast is a still-future world ruler who rises to great power during the tribulation.

Something to Ponder

One popular approach in the past was to look at the book of Revelation as a continuous record of events in history from John's day through the present day and up to the return of Jesus from heaven. The problem for these folks was to figure out which world events fit the events described in Revelation. No one could seem to get everything to fit!

Check Your Understanding

- **What is the preterist view of biblical prophecy?**

The preterist view is that the events described in the book of Revelation occurred in the first-century during the time of the Roman destruction of Jerusalem in AD 70. There is no future tribulation; it occurred in the past.

- **What is the futurist view of biblical prophecy?**

The futurist view is that the events described after chapter 4, verse 1 in Revelation are still in the future. The tribulation is a time of trial and judgment yet to come on the world.

Who Is Like the Beast?—His Character

You might get the idea from hearing him called "the Beast" that the Antichrist will be a raving, frothing-at-the-mouth lunatic! But that is not the case. *God* calls him the Beast because this term accurately describes his true character. While the world will hail the Antichrist as a great leader, a savior, God sees his inner nature and ambition.

In many respects the Antichrist will be the most remarkable political figure the world has ever seen. He will splash across the news headlines to unbelievable acclaim. He will be easy to like and even easier to follow.

First Impressions

Here is a peek at the Antichrist's biblical "résumé":

• *He will be wiser and more powerful than any other political leader in history.* People the world over will say, "Who is like the Beast? Who can make war against him?" (Revelation 13:4 NIV).

• *He will be a persuasive speaker and a cunning politician.* When he speaks, nations will be swayed by his words (Daniel 7:8; Revelation 13:5). He will even persuade the majority of people to worship him (Revelation 13:8).

The king will do whatever he wants. He will exalt and magnify himself above every god, and he will say outrageous things against the God of gods.

Daniel 11:36 HCSB

• *His political power and military strength will cause the whole world to stand in awe* (Revelation 13:3; 17:8). The Antichrist will succeed by war and by peace! He will give the impression that he has the answer to world peace

This lawlessness is already at work secretly, and it will remain secret until the one who is holding it back steps out of the way.

2 Thessalonians 2:7 NLT

by appearing to resolve several long-standing disputes, particularly in the Middle East.

His True Agenda

But as appealing as the Antichrist will seem on television and in the media reports of his accomplishments, he will have the inner character of a wild animal. He will embody pride, arrogance, and ambition like no one else ever has.

- *He will worship power.* Daniel said that he will "honor a god of fortresses" (Daniel 11:38 NIV). He will claim to be the most highly evolved being on the planet, worthy of the trust and obedience of everyone.

- *He will hate God.* The Antichrist will not be an atheist! He will admit that God exists, but he will hate God. His words will be venomous attacks on the character of God. The Antichrist will even proclaim himself to be the one god worthy of the world's worship (2 Thessalonians 2:4).

- *He will refuse to submit to any law but his own.* Simply put, the Antichrist will do as he pleases (Daniel 11:36). The apostle Paul called him "the lawless one" (2 Thessalonians 2:8 NIV). The only rebellion the Antichrist will not tolerate is rebellion against his own rule and authority. Those who dare to defy him will be crushed.

- *He will be the epitome of selfish ambition.* The Antichrist will appear humble and compassionate for a while, but ultimately he will exalt and magnify only himself. His self-exalting, proud attitude is the very heart of what it means to sin against God.

Held in Check

The Antichrist won't be the first political leader, of course, to defy God and to raise a fist in rebellion against God. The real power behind the Antichrist will come from Satan, who was the first being to turn away from God in defiance. The spirit of lawlessness and rebellion already permeates human society. You can see examples of it every day on your national or local news channel.

That *spirit* of antichrist is held in check at this point by God's Holy Spirit. The day will come, however, when the restraint of the Spirit is removed from human hearts. In the tribulation, God will remove the Spirit's control. The Spirit will not be taken out of the *world* at that point; the Spirit will be taken out of the *way*. The power of lawlessness was already at work in the first century to oppose God, but someone was holding back the full expression of humanity's desires. The person of lawlessness will not be revealed until after the restraining power of the Spirit is taken out of the way.

> Those who dwell on the earth will marvel . . . when they see the Beast.
>
> Revelation 17:8 NKJV

The Spirit will still be present in the world during the tribulation, but he will not restrain evil as he does now. Humanity's bent toward anarchy and lawlessness will be virtually unhindered (2 Thessalonians 2:7). The Antichrist will capitalize on that emerging spirit of unrestraint to cover his own abuse of power and his own domination of the world.

Something to Ponder

The word *antichrist* means a substitute Christ, a person who is totally the opposite of the true Christ and who is totally opposed to the true Christ. The Antichrist will come on the world scene as an acclaimed hero—a deliverer (a substitute Christ). But the Antichrist's goals will be oppression and personal power—the opposite of Jesus' goals!

Digging Deeper

Students of prophecy are divided over whether the Antichrist will be a Jew or a non-Jew (Gentile). Those who think the Antichrist will be a Jew base their conclusion on the assumption that the Jewish people will accept the Antichrist (for a while) as their promised Messiah. Those who think the Antichrist will be a Gentile point out that the Beast in Revelation 13:1 is said to come out of the sea. "The sea" is used frequently in prophetic visions to picture the nations of the world.

Points to Remember

• The Antichrist is a future ruler who will dominate the world during the seven-year tribulation period.

• The Antichrist will be empowered by Satan.

• The *power* of the Antichrist is at work in the world today; the *person* of the Antichrist will be revealed in the future when God no longer holds back Satan's evil plans.

Antiochus—An Ancient Foreshadowing of the Future Antichrist

Daniel is the Old Testament point man when it comes to prophecy. You may know him as the man who survived the lions' den, but he has a lot more on his résumé than that. In his prophecies and visions Daniel talked about an evil king who would oppress God's people and who would desecrate God's temple in Jerusalem. Four hundred years later just such a man walked out on the world scene and did exactly what God had predicted he would.

☧

Antiochus Epiphanes (an-tie´-o-cuss ee-pi´-fan-ees) was a Greek-speaking king who ruled over Syria (north of the land of Israel) between 175 and 163 BC. Antiochus invaded Israel in 168 BC and did his best to eradicate the worship of the Lord God. He told the Jews that they could not worship on the Sabbath. He prohibited circumcision, the observance of religious festivals, and the offering of animal sacrifices in the temple. Copies of the Hebrew Bible were burned, and Jews were ordered to eat pork (a meat prohibited by God's Law).

> The king shall do according to his own will: he shall exalt and magnify himself above every god, shall speak blasphemies against the God of gods, and shall prosper till the wrath has been accomplished.
>
> Daniel 11:36 NKJV
>
> He will start back to his own country and take out his anger on the religion of God's faithful people.
>
> Daniel 11:30 CEV

In what was the worst crime of all in the eyes of the Jews, Antiochus ordered that a pig (a ceremonially unclean animal) was to be offered as a sacrifice in God's temple. The sacrifice was dedicated to Zeus and to the new god-king, Antiochus himself.

A Jewish revolt, led by Judas Maccabaeus, eventually drove Antiochus and his army out of Israel. The temple was cleansed and the worship of

God was restored—an event Jewish people still celebrate each year at Hanukkah.

Daniel saw more in Antiochus than just an evil ruler. Antiochus was a foreshadowing of the future Antichrist. Both men would proclaim themselves to be gods; both would invade Israel; both would turn against the Jews who refused their new worship program; both would desecrate the temple in Jerusalem; and both would ultimately be destroyed.

Something to Ponder

Two-thirds of the prophecies in the book of Daniel have already been fulfilled—but the final third have yet to be fulfilled. The logic is simple: If part of Daniel's prophecies happened precisely as he predicted, it is safe to assume that the rest of Daniel's prophecies will take place in the future *just as precisely*. If his predictions about an evil Syrian king came true, it's not hard to believe that his predictions about a still-future evil king will also come true.

Digging Deeper

If you want to read more about Antiochus Epiphanes and about the future Antichrist in the book of Daniel, read Daniel 8:8-27 and 11:29-35. If you have access to a copy of the Apocrypha (you can find it online or in a Roman Catholic Bible), 1 Maccabees 1-6 is devoted to the story of the rebellion of godly Jews against the oppression of Antiochus.

"And the Nominees Are . . ."

Since the earliest years of the church, Christians have tried to figure out who the Antichrist might be. Some believe that Judas Iscariot, the disciple who betrayed Jesus, would be revived from the dead and become the Antichrist. Other early Christians were convinced that the Roman emperor Nero would return from the dead (or that he had never really died) and would emerge as the Antichrist. Neither of those men has appeared again in human history.

In every age Christians have continued to speculate about the identity of the Antichrist. Sometimes it has led to quiet supposition and at other times to loud accusation! Here is a list of some of the people down through history who have been identified as the Beast:

- Various Roman emperors
- Several popes and the papacy itself
- Emperor Frederick II and Pope Gregory IX (each of whom proclaimed the other to be the Antichrist)
- Martin Luther
- Napoleon I
- Each side in the American Civil War
- The League of Nations
- Adolf Hitler
- Joseph Stalin
- The United Nations
- Nikita Khruschev
- Yasser Arafat
- Saddam Hussein
- Henry Kissinger

Dear friends, do not believe every spirit, but test the spirits to determine if they are from God, because many false prophets have gone out into the world.

1 John 4:1 HCSB

Serve only the LORD your God and fear him alone. Obey his commands, listen to his voice, and cling to him.

Deuteronomy 13:4 NLT

- Several United States presidents—from both political parties—including Jimmy Carter, Ronald Reagan, John Kennedy, and George W. Bush.

And the list still goes on! Just go online or into a Christian bookstore and you will find someone who claims that he or she has figured out who the Antichrist really is.

Hint: Remember this list, and don't buy into their predictions!

It shouldn't surprise you that so many people have been labeled as a potential Antichrist. Satan doesn't know when Jesus will return either! So in every age he has to have a leader on the scene whom he could unveil as his anointed vessel. Most of the "candidates" listed above don't qualify to be the masterpiece of Satan, but somewhere just such a person stands ready.

Something to Ponder

Computers have always been prime candidates in some people's minds for the Antichrist. One math whiz figured out that if you give A the value of 6, B the value of 12, and so on, the letters of the word *computer* add up to "666"—the number of the Beast's name in Revelation 13:18. This idea picked up steam when employees at the European Common Market headquarters in Luxembourg affectionately nicknamed the central computer, "The Beast."

Myth Buster

When Mikhail Gorbachev was the leader of the old Soviet Union, speculation went wild among prophecy buffs that he was the Antichrist. Mikhail had a very prominent birthmark on his forehead that some people thought looked like a wound to his head. The Bible said that the Antichrist would survive a fatal wound  to his head—so (if you take a big enough leap) this was it! Gorbachev eventually had the outline of the birthmark protected by a trademark so a Russian company couldn't use it on their vodka label.

The Antichrist's Rise to Power

The Antichrist's evil character will not be revealed at first. He will come on the world scene as a wise deliverer, a skillful politician, and a firm decision-maker. During the first three and a half years of the tribulation, the Antichrist rises to power and extends his power over most of the Western world—Europe, the United States, and most of the Middle East. Then a crisis in Israel will launch the Antichrist to a whole new level of power and influence.

Here's how events in the early years of the tribulation will likely unfold. Not every student of prophecy will agree with every detail of the scenario, but things will generally go this way.

Out of Obscurity

Politically, the Antichrist will begin his career as a fairly inconspicuous person. He will probably be in a position of limited political power when the tribulation begins (although it's possible in today's world for a person to rise rather quickly from relative obscurity to great notoriety). The Old Testament prophet Daniel saw the Antichrist first appear on the world scene as "a little horn." It seems, then, that this leader will start out as a minor player on the political stage.

At the precise moment in God's plan, however, the Antichrist will begin to extend his power rapidly.

> Just as I was thinking about these horns, a smaller horn appeared, and three of the other horns were pulled up by the roots to make room for it.
>
> Daniel 7:8 CEV
>
> He will use every kind of evil deception. . . . So God will cause them to be greatly deceived, and they will believe these lies.
>
> 2 Thessalonians 2:10–11 NLT

Daniel predicted that the Antichrist would gain power within the context of the old Roman Empire. Some Bible teachers believe the Antichrist will rule over Europe (the area of the original Roman Empire). Others believe that he will rise to power in a Western nation (Europe or North America) and that he will eventually dominate the Western world—the part of the world that has basic cultural ties to the Roman Empire.

Ten Nations

Within a short period of time, the Antichrist will consolidate his political and military control over a ten-nation confederation. He may conquer some of these nations militarily, but, more likely, he will be given control because of his ability to resolve conflicts and govern with such skill. In Daniel's vision, the Antichrist rose in the context of ten small nations but soon overthrew three of them by military conquest (Daniel 7:8). The other seven simply fell under his sway politically, either voluntarily or by military threat. The ten-nation confederation will become the base for the Antichrist's political and military influence over other nations.

The world will be in a state of political turmoil when the Antichrist makes his appearance. Wars and threatened wars will add to the confusion. As judgments from God begin to sweep over the world in the early years of the tribulation, confusion and chaos will also sweep through the world's population. Conditions will be right for the rise of a strong leader. Desperate people will follow him without question. The Bible makes it clear that God will allow the vast majority of people living on earth to be deluded by this evil ruler. They will believe his lies.

The Antichrist will exercise his political control from a powerful, multi-nation confederation. He will set up a political dictatorship based on overwhelming military strength. At first the people under his authority will welcome his strong-handed control, but over time his rule will become more and more oppressive. The world will think for a time that peace and safety have finally arrived under the Antichrist's rule. They will learn quickly that his promise of peace comes at a very high price.

Treaty with Israel

In his new position of power, the Antichrist makes a treaty with the nation of Israel and guarantees Israel's security in the Middle East. He appears to solve the long-standing problems between Israel and her Arab neighbors. Israel proclaims the long-awaited arrival of peace. The people of Israel even begin to rebuild their temple, the center of worship to the Lord.

Surely your God is a God of gods and a Lord of kings and a revealer of mysteries, since you have been able to reveal this mystery.

Daniel 2:47 NASB

As the middle of the tribulation approaches, the Antichrist will have consolidated his power over the Western world and become Israel's protector. But events at the middle of the seven-year tribulation will push the Antichrist to a new level of ruthless oppression.

Something to Ponder

The belief that the Antichrist will rule over a ten-nation confederation is based on two images in biblical prophecy—the ten toes on the statue that King Nebuchadnezzar saw in a dream (Daniel 2:42–44) and the ten-horned Beast seen by both Daniel (Daniel 7:7–8) and the apostle John (Revelation 13:1). Daniel identified the ten toes as those kings who will be in power when God's kingdom arrives (Daniel 2:44). The ten horns on the Beasts in Daniel and Revelation also seem to be kings or kingdoms.

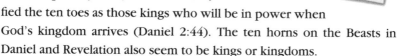

Myth Buster

Many prophecy writers have argued that the ten-horned Beast of Daniel and Revelation is fulfilled in the present-day European Union (or what used to be called the European Common Market). In 1973, the Union had nine members and, when Greece joined in 1981, prophecy buffs fully expected the Antichrist to make his way onto the stage of history. But soon the European Union expanded even more. The Antichrist's base of power will center on the old Roman Empire, but the European Union (at least in its present form) does not seem to be the fulfillment of what the prophets predicted.

Digging Deeper

Some interpreters of Revelation believe the ten-horned Beast that John saw was an image of the first-century Roman Empire. The ten horns (in this view) are the first ten Roman caesars. The problem comes when historians try to make a list of the first ten caesars. Some end up with twelve—or nine—caesars, but not ten.

The Mark of the Beast
(The Beast in God's Temple)

Near the midpoint of the seven-year tribulation, powerful nations will invade Israel. The Antichrist will use this threatened invasion as an opportunity to enter the land himself. He will defeat the opposing armies (called in Daniel 11 the king of the North and the king of the South) and will conquer the entire region of southwest Asia and northern Africa—the area commonly referred to as the Middle East.

The Antichrist will enter Israel as their deliverer and protector but, once he is there, he will refuse to leave—and then he will do something so shocking that the people of Israel will immediately realize that they have been betrayed!

The Antichrist will use his intervention in Israel as an opportunity to take the next step in his plan for world domination. He will enter the Jewish temple in Jerusalem and proclaim himself to be a god (2 Thessalonians 2:4)!

Wipe Out the Witnesses

The Antichrist will move quickly to eliminate all opposition to his newly claimed authority. He will not only hold political power, but he will also claim religious power. In the city of Jerusalem, two witnesses have been preaching the message of Jesus for three and a half years. These two men have been pointing out clearly that the Antichrist is an

> When you see the "abomination of desolation," spoken of by Daniel the prophet, standing in the holy place . . . then let those who are in Judea flee to the mountains.
>
> Matthew 24:15–16 NKJV

> The woman fled into the wilderness where she had a place prepared by God, so that there she would be nourished for one thousand two hundred and sixty days.
>
> Revelation 12:6 NASB

agent of Satan, not God. Up until this point, the Antichrist has just had to tolerate their words. Now, however, he will be in a position to do something about it.

The witnesses will pay for their testimony with their lives. Their bodies will lie in public view for three and a half days as the world looks on and celebrates (Revelation 11:7-10). The people of the world will blame all the judgments and plagues of the tribulation on these two preachers—and they will be happy to see them go. But after three and a half days, God will raise them from death and take them directly to heaven in a cloud (Revelation 11:11-13).

An Abomination

Meanwhile, back in the temple, the Antichrist will be constructing an image of himself as the object of the world's worship. The Antichrist will also introduce another powerful leader—the high priest of the Antichrist's new religion. This False Prophet will insist that every person under the Antichrist's rule worship the Beast and the image of the Beast standing in the temple.

Two groups will resist the Antichrist's efforts to spread his new religion—the followers of Jesus (many of whom have come to faith through the preaching of the two witnesses) and the Jewish people. The followers of Jesus will recognize the Antichrist's evil intentions from the very beginning. When the Jewish people see the Antichrist desecrate their temple with an image to be worshiped, they will finally recognize that he is a false leader and an enemy. Idolatry is one sin that Jewish people cannot tolerate.

Jesus warned the Jewish people that, when they saw "the abomination" (Daniel's word for the image of the Antichrist) standing in the temple, they were to run for their lives (Matthew 24:15-21). That act of rebellion and direct opposition to God's Law would mark the beginning of the days of great distress—the last three and a half years of the tribulation. Christians and Jews will flee the oppression of the Antichrist together—

and many will be protected by the Lord in the caves and crevasses of the Judean wilderness. God will open a way of escape for them and will supernaturally provide for them just as he provided for his people during the years of wandering in the days of Moses.

The two wings of the great eagle were given to the woman so that she could fly into the wilderness to her place.

Revelation 12:14 NASB

The world's perception of the Antichrist will change in the middle of the tribulation. Up until that point, he will have been hailed as a great leader and a shrewd politician. Now the real nature of the Beast will emerge. The Antichrist will demand the worship of every man and woman—and those who refuse to bow to his authority and to receive his mark will be pursued and eliminated.

Satan's goal since his original sin has been to be like God—worshiped like God, adored like God, loved and served like God. Satan's masterpiece will be the Antichrist, and for a while it will seem as if Satan has succeeded in gaining the worship that belongs only to God. But his whole plan will come crashing down!

Myth Buster

When the Bible says that the people of Israel (pictured as a woman) are given the wings of a "great eagle" (Revelation 12:14), some interpreters have taken that to mean the United States Air Force will carry out some kind of rescue airlift for those who are fleeing from the Antichrist's persecution. It is true that in the modern world the eagle is the symbol of the United States, but it seems more likely that John used the wings of a great eagle to picture the swiftness and silence of the Jews' escape into the desert.

Digging Deeper

Many students of prophecy believe that another modern nation will play a prominent role in end-times events—the nation of Russia. Several Old Testament prophets mention an attack on Israel "from the north" or "from the far north"—and Moscow is directly north of the Israeli city of Tel Aviv. In Ezekiel 38:2 a ruler is mentioned called "the prince of *Rosh*" (NASB, emphasis added)— and some readers have taken that to be a reference to Russia, but most scholars reject that identification.

Something to Ponder

Some interpreters (primarily Roman Catholic scholars) have identified the woman in Revelation 12 as Mary, the mother of Jesus. Other students of prophecy have made the case that the description goes beyond Mary and most likely represents the restored nation of Israel. It is a remnant of the nation of Israel that is preserved and protected in the wilderness for the last three and a half years of the tribulation.

The Beast Survives a Fatal Wound

In the course of his intervention and conquest of Israel in the middle of the tribulation, the Antichrist will be fatally wounded. Many interpreters believe that this will be an actual physical wound in the head, perhaps from an assassin's gun or a military attack. Other interpreters think it is a political "wound"—a challenge to the Antichrist's supremacy, which he is able to overcome. The Antichrist will die, or come close to death, but Satan, the enemy of God, will intervene and miraculously raise the Antichrist back to life.

✳

When President John Kennedy was assassinated by a sniper's bullet, rumors persisted for years that he was being kept alive in Dallas, Texas, and that he would be "revived" at some point and would emerge as the Antichrist. It was a ridiculous notion, of course, but that belief can be traced back to the statements in Scripture that the Antichrist will survive a fatal head wound.

In Revelation 13, as John described his vision of the Antichrist, he wrote, "One of the heads of the Beast seemed to have had a fatal wound, but the fatal wound had been healed. The whole world was astonished and followed the Beast" (v. 13:3 NIV). One element in the rise of the Beast to world power will be his survival of a fatal wound. He will be brought to the point of death or even killed by some violent means and then will be healed by Satan's power.

It worked for the Beast whose fatal wound had been healed. . . . Then it talked them into making an idol in the form of the Beast that did not die after being wounded by a sword.

Revelation 13:12, 14 CEV

The Beast which was and is not, is himself also an eighth . . . and he goes to destruction.

Revelation 17:11 NASB

As the world stands amazed at his miraculous recovery, the Antichrist will use the opportunity to take complete control of his empire by declaring himself to be a god! At that point, few people will be able to make much of an argument against him. No one before will have survived such a wound. It will be like the resurrection of Jesus—which is exactly what Satan will try to mimic when he revives the Antichrist.

Digging Deeper

In AD 68 the Roman emperor Nero was declared an enemy of Rome. He responded by committing suicide. But people had a hard time believing Nero had actually died. For years rumors circulated that he had not really died but had escaped to the Parthian Empire (east of Israel), where he was gathering a huge army to return and recapture his throne as Roman emperor. The legend became known as the *Nero redivivus* ("Nero revived") myth. Some early Christians held to that belief as well. They thought Nero would return as the Antichrist, the last evil ruler before the return of Jesus.

Something to Ponder

Rumors and speculation have always surrounded the subject of the Antichrist. Even the most mature Christians can, at times, be pulled into some strange ideas about who the Antichrist is or when he will appear. The safest place to stand is exactly where Scripture stands—no less than what Scripture teaches, but certainly no more either.

A Crashing End to an Evil Career—
The Defeat of the Antichrist

When the seven-year tribulation period comes to an end, the Antichrist will make his final attempt to destroy his enemies and defeat the purposes of God. His hatred will be focused primarily on two groups—the followers of Jesus and the Jews. The Jewish people will realize when the Antichrist sets up an image of himself in their beloved temple that he is a betrayer, and they will turn against him. But opposition is something the Antichrist will refuse to tolerate, and he will make it his mission to destroy these enemies of his evil reign. In the end, however, it will be the Antichrist who is destroyed.

Because of the Antichrist's incredible personal appeal, his miraculous powers, and his political and economic control, the world will fall at his feet in worship (Revelation 13:8). But some of the inhabitants of earth will refuse to worship this false Christ. The followers of Jesus, of course, will resist the Antichrist just as the early Christians resisted the commands of the Roman emperors to worship them as gods. The Jewish people as a whole will see the image of the Antichrist standing in the temple, and they will realize that he is not their deliverer but a liar. Both groups will be targeted for destruction.

The man of lawlessness will be revealed, but the Lord Jesus will kill him with the breath of his mouth and destroy him by the splendor of his coming.

2 Thessalonians 2:8 NLT

I saw Heaven open wide— and oh! a white horse and its Rider. The Rider, named Faithful and True, judges and makes war in pure righteousness.

Revelation 19:11 MSG

Jesus called the last three and a half years of the tribulation the "great tribulation" (Matthew 24:21 NASB). The Antichrist will be at the height of his power, and he will use that power to destroy any opposition. He will even attack the false religious system that had helped him rise to a place of such authority in the early years of the tribulation. The Beast will tolerate no worship but the worship directed at himself.

Men and women who resist the Antichrist will be hunted down, but those who support the Antichrist and receive his mark will face even greater trials. God's most punishing judgments will come on the earth in the last half of the tribulation. The universe will begin to shake loose as judgment after judgment pounds the earth and the people on it. People will crawl into caves and wish for death—anything to allow them to escape the outpouring of God's wrath.

Rumors from the East

The beginning of the end comes when the Antichrist hears reports of a massive army marching against him from the East—probably from China and India. Those parts of the world are the only areas not under the Antichrist's direct or indirect control (Revelation 9:13-16). The Antichrist will gather his own military forces in the land of Israel to meet the invading army. The war that follows is called the battle of Armageddon.

The Antichrist will either win this war or will persuade the armies from the East to join with him against the remnants of the Jewish people who are still alive in the land of Israel. The onslaught against the remnant of Israel and against the city of Jerusalem will be horrific.

Rescue from Heaven

When the situation looks most hopeless for Israel and for the followers of Jesus being pursued by the Antichrist, Jesus will return from heaven in power and glory and majesty (Matthew 24:29-31). The raptured and resurrected church will come with Jesus as his bride. The church won't do any fighting, but the inhabitants of the world will see a spectacular sight. The last act of the Antichrist will be his attack on the armies of the Lord (Revelation 19:19).

There really won't be much of a battle! Jesus will speak a word of judgment—one puff of his breath—and, like a giant sword, his spoken word will destroy his enemies (Revelation 19:15, 21). The vast armies gathered against God's people will collapse on the spot. The Antichrist will not be killed in this final war. He and his sidekick, the False Prophet, will be cast alive into a place of eternal torment (Revelation 19:20). The rest of his once powerful army will die, however, and the scavenging birds will eat their flesh (Revelation 19:21).

> The sign of the Son of Man will appear in the sky . . . and they will see the Son of Man coming on the clouds of heaven with power and great glory.
>
> Matthew 24:30 HCSB

The Antichrist's career will begin with such promise! He will appear on the world scene with the answers to some of society's most perplexing economic and political problems. The world will literally fall at his feet, but the evil intentions of his heart will soon become evident to all. In the end, he will come to a crashing end at the hand of the sovereign Lord of all, Jesus Christ.

Digging Deeper

Probably no Roman emperor embodied the character of the Antichrist like Nero (ruled from AD 54 to 68). He was a brutal, self-indulgent ruler who didn't hesitate to imprison or execute his enemies. Most of the Roman emperors were given divine honors after their deaths, but Nero claimed his before. He was depicted on coins as a god and allowed his statue to be set up in the Temple of Mars.

Points to Remember

• As the tribulation draws to a close, the Antichrist will focus his attention on wiping out his enemies—the followers of Jesus and the people of Israel.

• The Antichrist and his empire will be destroyed by the return of Jesus from heaven in magnificent glory.

Check Your Understanding

■ **What two groups will become the primary targets of the Antichrist's persecution?**

The followers of Jesus and the people of Israel.

■ **How will the Antichrist's career end?**

Jesus will return in majesty and destroy the armies of the Antichrist. The Antichrist will be cast alive into a place of torment.

■ **What are the dangers of trying to identify the Antichrist before God allows him to be revealed?**

All attempts at identifying the Antichrist up to this point have been wrong! Christians look for Christ, not for the Antichrist.

Satan's Role in the End Times

Some people think of Satan as a harmless little imp, a Halloween prankster. He may be around and create problems once in a while, but he's not important enough to worry about. Other people give Satan way too much power. They see him behind every bad experience and the cause of every pothole in the road. It's as though God and Satan are punching it out, and they aren't really sure who is going to win!

It is certainly dangerous to think of Satan as just a Halloween character. Satan is in fact a powerful angel who turned against God and set out on a course of rebellion against God. But don't give Satan too much power either. He is not equal with God—or even close. Satan operates only with God's permission. He was defeated forever by Jesus at the cross and the empty tomb. The war is over.

> Be of sober spirit, be on the alert. Your adversary, the devil, prowls around like a roaring lion, seeking someone to devour.
>
> 1 Peter 5:8 NASB

> That old snake and his angels were thrown out of heaven! That snake, who fools everyone on earth, is known as the devil and Satan.
>
> Revelation 12:9 CEV

When the future tribulation begins, God the Holy Spirit will take his hands off the wickedness in human hearts. Today human evil is restrained. As bad as it gets sometimes, it's not nearly as bad as it someday will be.

In the middle of the tribulation, Satan is cast out of heaven and confined to the earth (Revelation 12:7–13). His goal at that point will be to seek out and persecute as many believers in Jesus as he can. Satan will also try to destroy the people of Israel because God has promises yet to fulfill to Israel.

When Jesus returns in power at the end of the tribulation, Satan will be confined to a prison for spirits, the Abyss (Revelation 20:1–3). He will spend a thousand years in darkness and bondage. But then he will be released for a short time, and, after one final puny attempt at rebellion, Satan will be confined to the lake of fire forever (Revelation 20:10).

Digging Deeper

The New Testament refers to Satan with a variety of names and titles—none of them good!

- The devil (Matthew 4:1; 25:41 NIV)
- The serpent (2 Corinthians 11:3; Revelation 12:9; 20:2 NIV)
- The dragon (Revelation 12 NIV)
- Beelzebub (Matthew 10:25; 12:24, 27 NIV)
- The ruler of this world (John 12:31; 14:30; 16:11 NKJV)
- The evil one (Matthew 13:19; 1 John 2:13 NIV)
- The prince of demons (Matthew 9:34; 12:24 NIV)
- The accuser (Revelation 12:10 NIV)
- The enemy (Luke 10:19; 1 Peter 5:8 NIV)
- The prince of the power of the air (Ephesians 2:2 NASB)

Something to Ponder

While Satan is powerful and crafty, believers are not left defenseless against his attacks. Paul instructs Christians to put on the armor of God—spiritual resources for standing against evil, like truth and faith and prayer and the Word of God (Ephesians 6:11–18).

The Dragon Enters

Satan appears most often in the book of Revelation as a dragon. The apostle John saw a great wonder in the heavens—the appearance of an enormous red dragon (Revelation 12:3–4). Dragons are creatures of myths and fairy tales, but in this case the dragon pointed to another reality that John didn't want his readers to miss. The dragon represented a fierce evil being who stands opposed to God and who seeks to destroy God's plan for the salvation of humanity.

✳

John described the dragon/Satan in startling terms:

- *He was enormous, great, large*—a picture of Satan's power.

- *He was flame-colored, red*—the perfect color for his murderous intentions toward the people of God.

- *He had seven heads, seven crowns, and ten horns.* The heads, horns, and crowns clearly link Satan with the Antichrist's kingdom. Later in Revelation John portrayed the Antichrist in the same way (Revelation 13:1; 17:1). Satan will be the power behind the Antichrist.

Another Sign alongside the first: a huge and fiery Dragon! It had seven heads and ten horns, a crown on each of the seven heads.

Revelation 12:3 MSG

In that day the LORD with His severe sword, great and strong, will punish Leviathan [Satan] the fleeing serpent, Leviathan that twisted serpent.

Isaiah 27:1 NKJV

- *He was crowned with authority.* The crowns on the dragon's head were kingly crowns. For a while, at least, Satan will seem to hold ruling power over the earth.

- *He had great power.* Satan is not an enemy to be taken lightly. Jesus called him "the ruler of this world" (John 12:31; 14:30; 16:11 NKJV).

Satan certainly is not greater than God or more powerful than the Holy Spirit, who indwells the Christian, but Satan's power is not to be dismissed either.

Satan's single goal is to destroy the plan of God. If Satan can get God to compromise just a little, then Satan has become greater than God. So Satan through the Antichrist will seek to persecute the followers of Jesus. He will also seek to wipe out the people of Israel. John saw a vision of a woman giving birth to a child (Revelation 12:1-2, 5-6). Satan first tried to destroy the child (Jesus), but then turned his attention to the offspring of the woman (Israel) (Revelation 12:13-17).

Digging Deeper

The image of the dragon appeared in Old Testament scenes where evil powers and rulers threatened God's creation or God's people. Egypt, the great power defeated by God in the exodus, was described by Ezekiel as a dragon (Ezekiel 29:3-5; 32:2-8 MSG). The Old Testament always emphasized God's power over the dragon and his ability to defeat the dragon at every turn.

What Others Say

The dragon of John's vision would immediately be understood as the archenemy of God and his people.

Robert Mounce

The dragon did indeed kill Jesus. But what looked for all the world like Jesus' defeat turned out to be his victory because God raised him from the dead.

Paul Spilsbury

A Second Beast—The False Prophet

Satan does his best to imitate God—but only to accomplish evil, not good. In Revelation 13 three key figures form a satanic counterfeit of the Trinity. Satan is the mastermind, the real power. The second member of this corrupted trinity is the Antichrist, called the Beast out of the sea or the first Beast. Satan will give the Antichrist his power and his authority. The third person in the confederation is the False Prophet, called "another Beast." This man will be the Antichrist's right-hand man.

The Bible says that the second Beast will not come out of the sea, as the Antichrist had, but out of the earth (Revelation 13:11). Some scholars believe the phrase should be translated "out of the land," meaning out of the land of Israel. They conclude that the False Prophet will be Jewish, while the Antichrist will be a Gentile (non-Jew).

> [The second Beast] was allowed to put breath into the idol, so that it could speak. Everyone who refused to worship the idol of the Beast was put to death.
>
> Revelation 13:15 CEV

> False messiahs and false prophets will come and work miracles and signs. They will even try to fool God's chosen ones. But be on your guard!
>
> Mark 13:22–23 CEV

His Introduction

In the middle of the tribulation, the Antichrist will invade the land of Israel. He will come in as Israel's deliverer but will soon turn against the people. The Antichrist will enter the temple in Jerusalem and declare himself to be god. He will then construct (or unveil) an image of himself as the object of the world's worship. The Antichrist will also introduce another powerful leader—the high priest of the Antichrist's new religion.

His Power

The False Prophet (as this leader is later called) will exercise all the power and authority of the Antichrist and of Satan, the real power behind their rule. He will perform amazing miracles to demonstrate his power, and the people of the earth will be astonished at his capabilities. The False Prophet will even call down fire from heaven (Revelation 13:13). His miracles will not be miracles of good and healing, but miracles of deception, and the great majority of people will follow his instructions.

The False Prophet will oversee the placement of the image of the Antichrist in the temple, and he will somehow give breath or life to the image. The image will speak and demand the worship of the world's inhabitants (Revelation 13:15). The False Prophet will be the leader of this new world religion. No other religious system will be tolerated. Everyone from the poorest to the greatest will be required to worship the Antichrist and the image of the Antichrist. To refuse will mean certain death.

The False Prophet will also insist that every person under the Antichrist's authority receive a mark on their right hand or forehead. Without the mark no one will be able to hold a job, buy food, or avoid arrest and execution (Revelation 13:16-17). The False Prophet will bring powerful political, economic, and religious forces together to pressure the people of the earth into following his demands.

The Opposition

Two groups will resist the False Prophet's efforts to spread his new religion—the followers of Jesus and the Jewish people. The followers of Jesus will recognize the Antichrist's evil intentions from the very beginning. When the Jewish people see the Antichrist desecrate their temple with an image to be worshiped, they will finally recognize that he is a false leader and an enemy.

Jesus had warned the Jewish people that, when they saw "the abomination" (the prophet Daniel's word for the image of the Antichrist) standing in the temple, they were to run for their lives (Matthew 24:15–21). Anyone who refuses to worship the Beast or the image of the Beast will be executed. God will protect those who flee into the desert around Jerusalem, but many thousands will not heed Jesus' warning and will suffer the fatal consequences.

His Deception

The False Prophet will use several methods to deceive the people of the earth. He will perform *miracles* for political and economic reasons. He will bring a *gospel*, a message of deliverance, based not on Jesus'

> God will send upon them a deluding influence so that they will believe what is false.
>
> 2 Thessalonians 2:11 NASB

death and resurrection but on the Antichrist's survival of a fatal wound and his "resurrection" from the point of death (Revelation 13:12, 14). The second Beast will call down *fire from heaven,* perhaps in direct contrast to the fire that came from the mouths of the two godly witnesses of Revelation 11. The world will watch and listen and ultimately follow.

Myth Buster

The Bible uses the same words for Satan's miracles as it does for God's miracles! Satan's miracles are designed to lead people away from the truth, not toward it. Satanic miracles may involve magic, deception, and even demonic power. The False Prophet will be one source of evil spirits during the tribulation (Revelation 16:14), so it is not surprising that he can perform amazing works of power. The test of a miracle is not the miracle itself, but the source of the power behind the miracle.

The Two Beasts of Revelation 13

First Beast: The Antichrist	Second Beast: The False Prophet
Arises from the sea	Arises from the land
Military and political power	Religious and economic power
Survives a fatal wound	Ability to perform miracles
Persecutes God's people	Kills those who refuse to worship
Object of worship	High priest of worship

Points to Remember

- The False Prophet arises as the religious leader for the worship of the Antichrist.

- He has the ability to perform miracles in Satan's power, even giving "life" to the Antichrist's image.

- The Antichrist and the False Prophet will both be destroyed by one breath from Jesus Christ at his return in glory.

- Satan tries to imitate God, not to be good but to do evil.

- People will be amazed at what the False Prophet can do, and most people will follow his instructions.

- The False Prophet will insist that every person under the Antichrist's authority receive a mark on their right hand or forehead.

Worshiping the Beast

The first readers of the book of Revelation would have been familiar with several leaders who had exalted themselves as gods. In the Old Testament, the evil spiritual ruler of Babylon, Satan himself, had desired to be like God (Isaiah 14). Antiochus Epiphanes, a pagan Greek ruler in Syria, had demanded the worship of the Jewish people 150 years before Jesus was born (Daniel 11). Roman emperors like Caligula, Nero, and Domitian had been proclaimed to be gods by the Roman Senate and had demanded worship from the people in the Roman Empire.

The idea of a false prophet rising in Israel and leading God's people into idolatry was not an unknown concept either. Jeremiah (23) and Ezekiel (12-14) had both talked about religious leaders who would seek to deceive the people of Israel. So John's vision of a Beast from the sea (the Antichrist) who will demand worship and a Beast from the earth (the False Prophet) who will act as his priest was an idea not totally unheard of by the early Christians.

The cult of emperor worship was active in every city in the Roman world. Every citizen was required to offer a pinch of incense in worship to the emperor at least once a year.

There is only one God, the Father, who created everything, and we live for him.

1 Corinthians 8:6 NLT

The king will do as he pleases, and he will exalt and magnify himself above every god.

Daniel 11:36 NASB

It was a sign of loyalty to the emperor. As the incense was offered, the citizen said, "Nero (or whoever the current emperor was) is Lord." Christians, of course, could not say those words about anyone except Jesus. Jesus was their only Lord. So Christians refused to worship the emperor. Most of the time their refusal was ignored, but during the days when particular emperors strictly enforced the laws of emperor worship, Christians were persecuted and martyred for their refusal to worship their political leader.

The cult of caesar worship was enforced by priests throughout the empire. They demanded (like the False Prophet in Revelation 13) that Christians choose between two opposing confessions—Caesar is Lord or Jesus is Lord. Those who chose to confess Jesus as Lord often faced persecution or even death.

Digging Deeper

The New Testament emperors and their attitude toward emperor worship:

- Caesar Augustus (ruled 31 BC–AD 14) was deified after his death.
- Tiberius (14–37) had no interest in being worshiped.
- Caligula (37–41) revived the emperor cult.
- Claudius (41–54) refused emperor worship.
- Nero (54–68) demanded worship and persecuted Christians who refused.
- Vespasian (69–79) and Titus (79–81) ignored the emperor cult.
- Domitian (81–96) proclaimed himself divine ("Lord and God") and revived the imperial cult.

Something to Ponder

During the reign of Claudius, most Jews were exempt from offering incense to the emperor. Claudius did, however, expel Jews from Rome because (according to the historian Suetonius) they "were indulging in constant riots at the instigation of Chrestus." Some modern historians believe that is a reference to "Christus" or Christ and may indicate riots among the Jews between those who had believed in Jesus and those who refused to accept him as Messiah.

Rebuilding Israel's Temple

The New Testament says that the Antichrist will enter the temple and declare himself to be God (2 Thessalonians 2:4). That statement has presented a major problem to those who take prophecy seriously—there is no temple in Jerusalem today! On the basis of that prophecy, many Christians believe that the temple, the worship center of Israel, will be rebuilt—perhaps during the first part of the tribulation or even in the years before the tribulation begins.

A look at Israel's temple in the past will provide some perspective on the future:

- When Moses received the Ten Commandments and the Law, he also received instructions for constructing a portable worship center, called the *tabernacle*.

- Later in Israel's history, King Solomon built a permanent place of worship in Jerusalem—the *first temple*. It was finished in 960 BC.

- The *second temple* was begun after some of the Jews returned from captivity in Babylon in 536 BC. Almost five hundred years after that, Herod the Great began a massive expansion and beautification of the temple.

- The temple was destroyed in AD 70 by the Roman armies.

As He was going out of the temple complex, one of His disciples said to Him, "Teacher, look! What massive stones! What impressive buildings!"

Mark 13:1 HCSB

When Solomon finished praying . . . the glorious presence of the LORD filled the Temple.

2 Chronicles 7:1 NLT

- In AD 638, Muslim armies conquered Palestine. Muslims believe that the temple mount is the place where Muhammad was taken to heaven in a vision. In order to honor this sacred spot, a mosque and sacred complex (called the Dome of the Rock) was built.

That's the heart of the problem with a *third temple*. How can Israel build a temple on the same spot occupied by a Muslim mosque? Perhaps a compromise will be worked out, but it seems likely that a *tribulational temple* will be built. It is this temple that the Antichrist will take over as the center for the world's worship during the last half of the tribulation.

Something to Ponder

Christians today do not have a physical temple for worship. The Christian's body is a temple of the Holy Spirit (1 Corinthians 6:19) because the Holy Spirit dwells within each believer. When Christians gather for worship, whether it's in a church building or a house or a cave, the Holy Spirit makes that gathered group a temple for his own dwelling (1 Corinthians 3:16-17; Ephesians 2:21-22).

Check Your Understanding

- **Why do many Christians believe Israel's temple will be rebuilt?**

The Bible says that the Antichrist will enter God's temple during the tribulation and will exalt himself as God. Since Israel has no temple today, a temple will have to be rebuilt, and Jerusalem is the only place where God has authorized Israel to build one.

- **Are church buildings today the same as Israel's temple in the Old Testament?**

No. Church buildings are the places where God's people meet for worship, but the temple of God today is the body of the Christian believer because the Holy Spirit dwells in each Christian.

666–What It Means

When the False Prophet makes his appearance in the middle of the tribulation, he will insist that every person under the Antichrist's authority receive a mark on their right hand or forehead (Revelation 13:16–17). *The mark of the Beast* has become a universal symbol of terror and oppression—but what is it? John said that a *mark* (the word means a "brand" as in branding cattle or even a "tattoo") would be placed on every person who worships the Beast. It will be a visible sign of a person's allegiance to the Antichrist.

The mark is also an access code that will permit the person to conduct the responsibilities of life—get a job, buy food, get a driver's license—*and* avoid arrest and execution! Anyone without the mark will be hunted down. While most of those who refuse the mark of the Beast will die physically in the tribulation, those who compromise and take the mark will suffer the eternal wrath of God (Revelation 14:9-11; 16:2; 19:20). Accepting the mark will seal a person's doom forever.

If anyone . . . receives a mark on his forehead or on his hand, he also will drink of the wine of the wrath of God.

Revelation 14:9–10 NASB

A foul and loathsome sore came upon the men who had the mark of the Beast and those who worshiped his image.

Revelation 16:2 NKJV

John added one more puzzling element to his description of the Beast's mark. The mark will be the name of the Beast or the number of his name. John then says, "His number is 666" (Revelation 13:18). John was probably referring to the ancient practice of assigning a number to various letters of the alphabet and then calculating the "number" of a person's name.

The Antichrist's name computes to 666—but what numerical system is being used? And what language? Christians have found "666" everywhere! Almost every year someone claims to have "discovered" how a prominent person's name adds up to 666. Sometimes the name has to be translated into Hebrew or Greek in order to get the math to come out right.

It's most likely that no one will know how this 666 thing works until the mark begins to be branded on people's hands and foreheads. It will be obvious then, but right now it's still a mystery.

Final Thoughts

 John's original audience would have been familiar with image worship. Not long before Revelation was written, the emperor Domitian had a statue of himself erected in Ephesus that stood more than twenty feet tall. The word John used for the "mark" of the Beast was also used for the emperor's seal on business contracts and for his image on Roman coins. The mark denoted loyalty and ownership.

Something to Ponder

The book of Revelation saw two powers at war with no neutral territory between them. Men and women give allegiance either to the Beast or to God. They have to choose. Their loyalty is reflected primarily through what they choose to worship.

Computers, Credit Cards, and Other Suggestions

When Social Security numbers began to be issued to every United States citizen, some Christians were convinced that the mark of the Beast had come. Internal Revenue forms, retail store bar codes, credit cards, and even Internet addresses have at one time or another been pointed to as "the mark." The Antichrist will certainly use whatever means are available to him to pursue his goal of total control over every person and over every facet of life, but some of the suggestions for his "mark" are ridiculous.

A few proposals for the "mark of the Beast":

- The escalating use of credit cards has been widely regarded by prophecy buffs as the first step toward a universal money card that the Antichrist will use to control all buying and selling.

- Computers have made the threat of absolute control over income and spending more of a possibility. One writer figured out that if you give A the value of 6, B the value of 12, and so on, the word "computer" adds up to 666! (By the way, "Mark of the Beast" and "New York City" also add up to 666 in that system.)

Here is wisdom: The one who has understanding must calculate the number of the Beast, because it is the number of a man. His number is 666.

Revelation 13:18 HCSB

God's holy people must endure persecution patiently, obeying his commands and maintaining their faith in Jesus.

Revelation 14:12 NLT

- Some Amish groups in Indiana moved to Iowa in the mid-1960s because the state government required them to put an orange triangle warning sign on the back of their horse-drawn buggies. They saw the intrusion as "the mark of the Beast."

• Ronald Wilson Reagan was tagged as the Antichrist because he had six letters in each of his three names—or 6/6/6. Do you really think that the apostle John had the English language in mind when he wrote this at the end of the first century?

• In 1956 one Bible teacher confidently declared that John F. Kennedy was the Antichrist because he received 666 votes at the Democratic presidential convention.

Speculation about how the number 666 fits into the name and identifying mark of the Antichrist will always be around. If you are tempted to take a suggestion seriously, just remember this list!

Something to Ponder

The mark of the Beast is always deliberately received in Revelation; it is not something a person will receive by accident. People must choose to accept the mark of the Beast or choose to reject it out of loyalty to Christ. Christians will not be "tricked" or deceived into accepting something that will later be revealed as the mark of the Antichrist.

Digging Deeper

Some interpreters of Revelation do not think that the "mark of the Beast" or "the seal of God" will be literal, visible marks but are to be understood in a figurative sense. Receiving the mark of the Beast implies a willingness to ally oneself with the powers that oppose Christ. In the same way, receiving the seal of God on the forehead implies an unswerving allegiance to Jesus.

A False Church Rises and Falls

The Antichrist and the False Prophet will use two avenues of power to place a stranglehold on the people under their domination—religious worship and economic control. Both the religious system and the economic system are called *Babylon* in the Bible. It's a title that looks back to the Old Testament where "Babylon" was viewed as the source of all false worship and idolatry. After the great flood early in earth's history, humankind disobeyed God's command to fill the earth. God confused human language and forced human beings to disperse over the earth. That place was later called Babylon.

Religious Babylon in the tribulation will include all corrupt and false religious systems. Early in the tribulation period, an apostate "church" will emerge. The word *apostate* means "to stand away from" the place where you once stood. In biblical language, an apostate is one who stands outside true faith in Jesus. It's possible that the False Prophet will be the leader of this false religious system.

The ten horns which you saw on the Beast, these will hate the harlot, make her desolate and naked.

Revelation 17:16 NKJV

The Holy Spirit tells us clearly that in the last times some will turn away from the true faith.

1 Timothy 4:1 NLT

The False Church on the Rise

The apostle John was invited by an angel to witness the downfall of "the great prostitute" (Revelation 17:1 NIV). Based on what John saw in Revelation 17, several conclusions can be drawn about how the apostate religious system got started.

• The future false "church" will permeate the Antichrist's empire. Everybody will be touched by the false religious system's power (Revelation 17:15).

- The apostate religious Babylon will link its power to the political power of the Beast. The kings of the earth will get in bed with the religious prostitute and commit immorality with her (Revelation 17:2). That is the Bible's vivid way of describing spiritual unfaithfulness to God.

- The future false church becomes an instrument of deception in the Antichrist's hand. The Antichrist will use the religious influence of the false church to draw people to his side (Revelation 17:3). The goal of evil people in the tribulation will be to exalt their hero. Just as Christians want glory and honor to go to Jesus, those who follow the prostitute church will give up everything for the Antichrist.

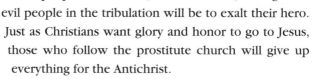

- The false church is not only powerful but also fabulously wealthy. John saw a woman dressed in scarlet and purple—expensive colors to produce in the ancient world. Gold, precious stones, and pearls were hanging from her neck and wrists (Revelation 17:4).

- The false church will also persecute the true followers of Jesus. When John saw her, she was drunk with the blood of God's people, the blood of those who bore testimony to Jesus (Revelation 17:6).

The False Church Destroyed

John also gave his readers a clue about the center of the Antichrist's power during the tribulation. He said that the Beast on which the prostitute church rode had seven heads and the seven heads were seven hills on which the woman sat (Revelation 17:9). For centuries before John wrote this, Rome was known as the seven-hilled city. The religious and political center of the Antichrist's empire will be the city of Rome.

In the first half of the tribulation, the prostitute church will gain unbelievable power and influence. But the day will come when the Antichrist and his political allies will tear religious Babylon to shreds. It seems likely that the false church is destroyed in the middle of the tribulation. When the Antichrist sets himself up as God in the temple, he will tolerate no competition, no rivalry for worship. At that point he will strip the apostate church of her power and devour her wealth.

The Antichrist will think he is accomplishing his own purposes in destroying religious Babylon, but in reality he will be doing God's will. The Beast and his allies will end up hating the prostitute, but by their actions they will accomplish God's purposes. The one in control is *not* Satan or the Antichrist; the one in control of a world that seems out of control is a sovereign God.

> Don't be naive. There are difficult times ahead.
>
> 2 Timothy 3:1 MSG

The false church of the future will seek power by making an alliance with the Antichrist—and for a while the plan will succeed. The prostitute church will think she can control the Antichrist, but she will find out too late that he has used her for his own ends. The Beast will take all that he can and then will smash the false church in hatred and rage.

Digging Deeper

The ancient city of Rome was built on seven hills near the Tiber River. Their names echo through Rome's long history—Palatine, Aventine, Caelian, Esquiline, Viminal, Quirinal, and Capitoline. Other hills were added as the city expanded, but Rome was always known as "the city of seven hills." The title was used repeatedly by 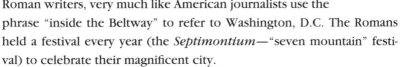 Roman writers, very much like American journalists use the phrase "inside the Beltway" to refer to Washington, D.C. The Romans held a festival every year (the *Septimontium*—"seven mountain" festival) to celebrate their magnificent city.

What Others Say

While the Beast is the political ruler of the empire, the woman represents the blasphemous religion that seduces the nations.

Grant Osborne

The New Testament is clear in its warning about the dangers of apostasy in every generation but especially in the last days before the rapture of the church.

Mal Couch and Ed Hindson

Points to Remember

- A universal false religious movement will rise to great power in the first of the tribulation.

- The apostate "church" will exalt the Antichrist and persecute followers of Jesus.

- In the middle of the tribulation, the Antichrist will destroy the prostitute religion—and exalt himself as God.

The Destruction of the Antichrist's Empire

Babylon is a term used in the book of Revelation to refer to the Antichrist's empire in all its forms. It's a code word for all that stands against God. The Beast will rule over an entire system—political, religious, economic, cultural—that is based on hatred toward God. The Antichrist will not be an atheist; he will acknowledge that God exists, but he will despise God and oppose God's plan in every way possible.

The Antichrist's power will center in one magnificent city. The apostle John calls it "Babylon the Great" (Revelation 18:2 NIV). The city will be the capital of the Antichrist's revived Roman Empire. It will be the focus of world attention over the seven years of the tribulation, but with one stroke, God will destroy the city. Babylon will fall because her sins are piled up to heaven and because God remembers her crimes.

Three groups will be devastated by Babylon's fall:

> How terrible, how terrible for you, O Babylon, you great city! In a single moment God's judgment came on you.
>
> Revelation 18:10 NLT
>
> You rich people are in for trouble. You have already had an easy life!
>
> Luke 6:24 CEV

• First, *the kings of the earth,* the political leaders who escape the city's collapse, will weep and mourn for their destroyed empire. Their strength and influence will be gone (Revelation 18:9-10).

• The second group to mourn for Babylon will be the *merchants*. They will be upset because their wealth will be gone (Revelation 18:11-17). The things people think are so important will mean nothing when God's judgment falls.

• *Seamen* who earn their living transporting goods to Babylon will cry too. They will have become rich because of Babylon, but now their jobs will be gone forever.

Some students of prophecy believe that the Antichrist's city will be destroyed by a nuclear attack because there is so much devastation in such a short time. But the Bible links Babylon's destruction to the direct judgment of God (Revelation 18:8).

Digging Deeper

The marks of the Antichrist's "Babylon" include the following:

- • Rich and prosperous (Revelation 17:4)
- • Closely connected to Satan and the Beast (17:7-8)
- • A city that rests on seven hills (17:9)
- • An empire that rules over many peoples (17:15-18)
- • The center of international commerce (18:3, 11-13)
- • Dependent on supplies from sea merchants (18:17-18)
- • An entertainment and pleasure capital (18:22-23)
- • Destroyed by fire in one hour (18:9-10, 17, 19)

Something to Ponder

God calls any believers living in the doomed city of Babylon to come out before judgment falls (Revelation 18:4). When a society or nation is too corrupt to listen to God, judgment soon follows. But before judgment comes, God warns his people to leave. Those who fail to heed God's warning will share in its destruction.

Where in the World Is Babylon?

One of the most significant questions in biblical prophecy centers on the term *Babylon.* Some interpreters believe it is a reference to the literal city of Babylon on the Euphrates River in modern Iraq. Originally, Babylon was the place where God confused human language after the flood (Genesis 11). It was first called *Bab-El* (meaning "gate of God"), but God called it *Babel* (meaning "to confuse"). Later, the city was called Babylon. Other prophecy students believe Babylon is used in a symbolic way, as a code for another city. It might help to look at the arguments on both sides.

Those who believe that Babylon in the book of Revelation refers to the literal city in Iraq make the following points:

- The Bible says "Babylon"—and if Scripture is to be interpreted in its normal sense, Babylon should be Babylon.

- God predicted the destruction of Babylon in the Old Testament, but those predictions have yet to be *completely* fulfilled (see Isaiah 13 and 47; Jeremiah 50–51; and Zechariah 5).

- The ancient city of Babylon will be rebuilt as a magnificent city and will become the political and economic center of the Antichrist's empire—all within the years leading up to the tribulation or early in the tribulation.

Ruined, ruined, Great Babylon, ruined! A ghost town for demons is all that's left!

Revelation 18:2 MSG

Babylon . . . will be as when God overthrew Sodom and Gomorrah. It will never be inhabited.

Isaiah 13:19–20 NKJV

Those who believe that the word *Babylon* refers to another city rely on other arguments:

- The Old Testament predictions of Babylon's fall *were* fulfilled when the Persians conquered and later destroyed the city. Attempts at rebuilding the city have all failed.

- Rebuilding the actual city of Babylon would take decades.

- John indicated that he didn't want his readers to take "Babylon" as a reference to the city in Iraq. He called it "mystery Babylon" (Revelation 17:5 NIV).

- Babylon in Revelation sits on seven hills (17:9)—a clear reference to the city of Rome.

- The Antichrist will rule over a revived Roman/Western empire from a powerful city. John calls it "Babylon" as a code word for Rome.

Digging Deeper

Some Christians do not think John was referring to a *future* city of Rome in Revelation but to the *ancient* city of Rome. A coin was minted in AD 71 in Asia Minor that depicts the goddess Roma sitting across the seven hills of Rome. This image was an obvious way of depicting the Roman Empire in John's day, and his readers would have recognized it as such.

Something to Ponder

The term *Babylon* is used one other place in the New Testament to refer to Rome. At the end of his first letter, the apostle Peter wrote, "She who is in Babylon, chosen together with you, sends you her greetings, and so does my son Mark" (1 Peter 5:13 NIV). Neither Peter nor Mark were ever associated with the literal city of Babylon, but both were in the city of Rome.

Angels in the End Times

Satan is not the only angel to play a prominent role in the wrap-up of human history. God's holy angels also play a part. In almost every scene of end-times prophecy, angels appear, announce, warn, hurl stones, or blow trumpets. They will shout with the millions of redeemed believers in heaven and will sweep through the world on missions of judgment. Angels are not cute little babies with wings that adorn Valentine's Day cards; they are mighty, majestic messengers of God.

✳

Here are a few of the places in end-times prophecy where holy angels play a significant role:

- The apostle John saw a magnificent scene of worship in heaven in Revelation 4 and 5. Surrounding God's throne were four living creatures—powerful angels who exalted the holy character of God day and night (Revelation 4:6–8).

- Tens of thousands of angels surround God's throne in heaven and join with the redeemed people of God in giving praise and honor and blessing to the Lamb (Revelation 5:11–12).

- Angels will seal the 144,000 witnesses from Israel with the protection of God (Revelation 7:1–8).

- Seven angels will blow the seven trumpets that will release waves of judgment on the earth in the middle of the tribulation (Revelation 8–10).

- A mighty angel gave the apostle John a little scroll to eat and encouraged John in his ministry as a prophet (Revelation 10).

> I saw the Lord sitting on his throne with all the armies of heaven around him, on his right and on his left.
>
> 1 Kings 22:19 NLT
>
> When the Son of Man comes in His glory, and all the angels with Him, then He will sit on the throne of His glory.
>
> Matthew 25:31 HCSB

- Seven angels will pour out the bowls of God's wrath on the earth at the end of the tribulation (Revelation 15-16).

- Angels will move through the earth at Jesus' return in glory to remove unbelievers (Matthew 13:41-42).

- An angel gave John a tour of the future eternal city of Jerusalem (Revelation 21:9).

- The same angel rebuked John for worshiping him and commanded him to worship God alone (Revelation 22:8-9).

Digging Deeper

The angel Michael is usually pictured in Scripture as the military angel, the protector of Israel (Daniel 12:1; Revelation 12:7). In the middle of the tribulation he will gather the holy angels under his command and wage war with Satan and the evil angels who have linked themselves to God's enemy. Michael is also called "the archangel" in Jude 9 (NIV).

Something to Ponder

Angels are such powerful beings that human beings are tempted to fall before them in worship. At that point, the angel is tempted to receive that worship and to follow Satan down the path of desiring to be like God. Holy angels immediately intervene and encourage the believer to worship God and only God.

The Last World War—
The Battle of Armageddon

The forces of evil will make one last stand against the Lord and against his people as the tribulation comes to an end—and then Jesus will return in power!

Contents

Multitudes, multitudes in the valley of decision! For the day of the LORD is near in the valley of decision.

Joel 3:14 NKJV

The Battle Plan

If you thought that the world was going to be spared from Armageddon because Bruce Willis blew up that asteroid just in time, you are sadly mistaken! (You will have to rent or download the 1998 movie *Armageddon* if you don't get the asteroid thing.) The word *Armageddon* has come to mean "the end of the world" in popular jargon. The word actually comes from the Bible, and it isn't the end of the world—but it does change everything.

✳

The Place

Armageddon is a Hebrew word that means "hill of Megiddo." You will find the word only once in the Bible. In Revelation 16, evil spirits go out to the rulers of the entire world to bring them together for battle. The armies gather at a place called Armageddon (vv. 14, 16).

The hill of Megiddo overlooks a wide, fertile plain called the plain of Esdraelon (ez´-dra-lon), or the valley of Jezreel. The Bible pinpoints that area as the location of the final battle of the great day of the Lord. The plain of Esdraelon is located in the northern part of the land of Israel about twenty miles southeast of present-day Haifa.

The LORD will attack those nations like a warrior fighting in battle. He will take his stand on the Mount of Olives.

Zechariah 14:3–4 CEV

I saw the Beast and the kings of the earth and their armies assembled to make war against Him who sat on the horse and against His army. And the Beast was seized.

Revelation 19:19–20 NASB

The Play-by-Play

Here's how the events will likely unfold:

- At the midpoint of the tribulation the Antichrist will invade the land of Israel and declare himself to be a god. He will demand the world's worship and allegiance.

- The nations of the East that are not under the Antichrist's direct control (nations like China, India, and the nations of central and Southeast Asia) will agree together to march against the armies of the Antichrist. The Antichrist's threat of world domination will be greater than the religious and political issues that have divided these nations for centuries.

  - A massive army of two hundred million people then will begin to move from the East toward the Antichrist's new location in Jerusalem. Even God will help prepare the way for this army by drying up the Euphrates River (Revelation 16:12-21).

- When this enormous army reaches the area of Israel, the Antichrist will have already assembled his own army near the wide plain of Esdraelon.

- The battle that follows will be devastating—and it will spread quickly to engulf the whole region. Blood from human beings and from animals will literally flow like a stream through the valley (Revelation 14:17-20).

- The Antichrist apparently will emerge victorious over the armies of the East. It is also possible that all the armies will simply decide to join forces against Jesus Christ, who is about to return to earth.

- The Antichrist will turn his forces against the Jewish people still living in the land of Israel. Many of them will die in the Antichrist's attack, but God will save a small group, a remnant of the nation, who will escape from Jerusalem and who will be protected by God in the wilderness.

The Powerful Victory

The battle scene will cover an area of two hundred miles north to south and one hundred miles east to west. Into that area multiplied millions of soldiers and civilians will be crowded for the final war. Rulers with their armies will come from east and north and south. Demons will rise up to spur men and women on in their desire for conquest. But at the last moment, an invasion from heaven changes everything.

> I will pour on the house of David and on the inhabitants of Jerusalem the Spirit of grace . . . then they will look on Me whom they pierced.
>
> Zechariah 12:10 NKJV

Just when it seems that the Antichrist will destroy once and for all the people of Israel as well as the followers of Jesus, Christ will return from heaven in brilliant glory and awesome power as God's Great Warrior. He will destroy the armies of the Antichrist with one word of command, one breath of his mouth.

The surviving Jews in Israel will recognize Jesus as their true Messiah and will turn to him in repentance and faith. Israel's turning to Jesus in faith will also bring about the fulfillment of God's promise to make a new covenant with Israel (see Ezekiel 36:24-28 and Jeremiah 31:31-34). Jesus will be welcomed as Israel's Deliverer when he comes again in majesty.

Then Jesus will take his place as King over the whole earth, as he removes wickedness and ushers in a kingdom of peace.

Digging Deeper

The plain of Esdraelon is a triangular valley bounded by mountain ranges and the Mediterranean Sea. The city of Nazareth, where Jesus grew up, is located on the northern rim of the valley. Jesus would often have looked out over this valley as he scanned south toward the city of Megiddo.

Some of the fiercest battles of the Old Testament were fought in this valley—Gideon's victory over Midianite invaders (Judges 7); King Saul's defeat by the Philistines (1 Samuel 31); King Josiah's defeat by the Egyptians (2 Kings 23:29). It will also be the scene of the first battle in a great war at the end of the tribulation—the battle of Armageddon.

Points to Remember

- Armageddon will be the last great war in human history. It begins at the end of the seven-year tribulation period.

- The Antichrist will try to exterminate the Jews who are living in the land of Israel.

- Jesus will return from heaven in glory and power to destroy the Antichrist and the armies of the world.

Myth Buster

The Bible's description of the battle of Armageddon implies that soldiers will be on horseback and will use ancient weapons in hand-to-hand combat. Can this be an accurate description of a war still in the future?

Two possible explanations:

1. The devastating wars earlier in the tribulation and the judgments of God on the earth will have effectively destroyed humanity's ability to use modern technology.

2. It's also possible that the biblical writers were trying to describe modern weapons with an ancient vocabulary. They simply had no word for tank or cruise missile!

Warnings in the Old Testament

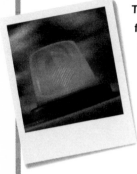

The Old Testament prophets spoke repeatedly about the final battle of the tribulation. They saw it as the great climax of humanity's rebellion against God and the ultimate response of God to that rebellion. Human beings may devise all kinds of plans against the Lord and against his people—and sometimes those plans seem to succeed! But in the end, the rebellion of the nations against God will be crushed by the appearance of Jesus Christ, the Warrior of the Lord.

✳

Here's a list of the key passages on Armageddon in the Old Testament and a summary of what they teach:

- *Psalm 2.* The psalmist contrasted the proud boasts of the world's rulers with the awesome majesty and power of the Lord. God laughs at human insolence!

- *Isaiah 34:1-15.* Isaiah used the coming destruction of Israel's enemies, particularly the Edomites, to picture the Lord's vengeance on the rebellious nations.

- *Isaiah 63:1-6.* The Lord is portrayed as a mighty warrior, robed in splendor and walking in strength. The armies of the world will fall before his power. This passage is also the biblical text from which the Civil War song "The Battle Hymn of the Republic" was drawn.

- *Joel 3:1-17.* This passage depicts the Lord's protection of the people of Israel in the day of his vengeance on the world.

In that day the LORD will defend the inhabitants of Jerusalem; the one who is feeble among them in that day shall be like David, and the house of David shall be like God.

Zechariah 12:8 NKJV

Who is this in royal robes, marching in his great strength? "It is I, the LORD, announcing your salvation! It is I, the LORD, who has the power to save!"

Isaiah 63:1 NLT

- *Zechariah 12:1-9.* Zechariah echoed Joel's promises of the Lord's protection of Israel. The nations of the world will stumble over the city of Jerusalem.

- *Zechariah 14:12-16.* Zechariah graphically pictured the plague that the Lord will use to destroy the armies of all those who come against the city of Jerusalem in that future battle.

- *Malachi 4:1-3.* Malachi emphasized the joy of God's people when they see the deliverance of the Lord.

Digging Deeper

The Bible refers to the last great war with several titles of judgment (NIV):

- "A day of vengeance" (Isaiah 34:8)
  - "The winepress" of God's anger (Isaiah 63:2; Joel 3:13; Revelation 14:19-20)
- "The great and dreadful day of the LORD" (Joel 2:31; Malachi 4:5)
- "The harvest" (Joel 3:13; Revelation 14:15-16)
- "The great day of God Almighty" (Revelation 16:14)

Something to Ponder

Christians have different views of the battle of Armageddon based on their general approach to biblical prophecy. Students of prophecy who believe that the tribulation prophecies were fulfilled when Rome destroyed Jerusalem in AD 70 see the battle of Armageddon as the decisive battle in which Roman troops broke into the city of Jerusalem and began the process of executing the inhabitants. Christians who view the book of Revelation as a symbolic picture of the constant struggle between good and evil interpret the battle of Armageddon as the final triumph of Jesus Christ over all the evil forces in the universe.

Israel Restored

The modern State of Israel came into existence in 1948. This reemergence of the nation after two thousand years of exile had a huge impact on the interpretation of biblical prophecy. Before the nation was reestablished, most Christians assumed that the Old Testament prophecies about a restored Israel in the land God had given Abraham were to be understood in a symbolic or spiritual way. When the literal State of Israel came into being, however, many Christians began to give new consideration to the way the Old Testament prophecies were to be interpreted.

Probably the most popular view among Christians in the United States and Canada is that the creation of the modern State of Israel is a literal fulfillment of Old Testament prophecy. The creation of a political state in the Land of Promise is also seen as a sign that the end times are drawing near. With the emergence of Israel, the world stage is set for the unfolding of the events of the book of Revelation.

Other Christians take differing views. Some believe that the modern State of Israel may or may not have a role to play in the end times. They say that, just as Israel was disobedient to God in the past and lost the land, modern Jews have gathered in Israel in unbelief and so may lose the land again. Who is to say that God won't judge Israel again as he did in the past for their lack of justice or right relationship with their Messiah?

"Behold, days are coming," declares the LORD, "when I will fulfill the good word which I have spoken concerning the house of Israel and the house of Judah."

Jeremiah 33:14 NASB

When this happens, ten people . . . will grab a Jew by his clothes and say, "Let us go with you. We've heard that God is on your side."

Zechariah 8:23 CEV

Still other Christians do not see any role for political Israel in the end times. They believe that, because of Israel's unbelief in the past, God has transferred the promises given to Old Testament Israel to the "new Israel," the church. The formation of the nation of Israel, in their view, has no bearing at all on the interpretation of biblical prophecy.

Myth Buster

When the nation of Israel was formed in 1948, some prophecy students believed that a prophetic clock began to tick. They based their excitement on Jesus' words in Mark 13:30 where Jesus promised that "this generation will certainly not pass away until all these things have happened" (NIV). Since a biblical "generation" was about forty years, there were many Christians who anticipated that the Lord would return before 1988—one generation after 1948. Several prophecy preachers wrote books and made predictions as 1988 approached, but the year passed without the rapture or the return of Christ.

Further Insight

Many of the Old Testament prophets encouraged the people of Israel with wonderful promises about a future "golden" age when the Messiah would reign:

• A new "exodus" would take place. The people of Israel would return from every place where they had been scattered (Isaiah 43:5-6).

• The lame, the blind, and the weak will be included (Jeremiah 31:8; Micah 4:6-7).

• Jerusalem will be rebuilt, and a just king of the family of David will reign (Zechariah 14:16).

The Surprising Final Victory

No television crime story or spy thriller novel could end with a more heart-stopping climax! The Antichrist and his armies have engulfed the land of Israel and surrounded the city of Jerusalem. Millions of Jews and followers of Christ have been killed. It seems the darkest of days for the survivors. Just at the moment when everything seems lost, the entire scene changes. The heavens open and a majestic person appears. God himself is coming to earth!

The Words of His Coming

In the Greek language of the New Testament, three different words are used to describe Jesus' personal return to earth in the future. The words give you some insight into what the second coming of Christ involves.

All three words are used of both Jesus' coming in the rapture for his church and Jesus' return in power with his church.

Stay with Christ. Live deeply in Christ. Then we'll be ready for him when he appears, ready to receive him with open arms.

1 John 2:28 MSG

Rest your hope fully upon the grace that is to be brought to you at the revelation of Jesus Christ.

1 Peter 1:13 NKJV

• The word *parousia* means "presence" or "arrival." Jesus' coming will involve his personal presence. At the rapture, Christians will see Jesus in the air and will meet him in the air. At his return, the whole world will see the one they have mocked and scorned arriving in majesty. The word was used in the ancient world of the arrival of a king or ruler, and it is used in the Bible of the arrival of the King of all kings. This word is used many times in the New Testament, including Matthew 24:3 and 1 Thessalonians 3:13 and 4:15.

- The word *apocalypsis* means "unveiling" or "revealing." When Jesus returns he will be revealed as God's unique Son, the Creator and Judge of all. People may ignore Jesus today, but, when that day comes, no one will escape the truth of who Jesus is. This word is not used as often as *parousia* to describe Christ's coming, but it is used in places like 1 Corinthians 1:7 and 1 Peter 1:13. The book of Revelation is called an "apocalypse" in Revelation 1:1—the unveiling of Jesus as he really is.

- The third word is *epiphaneia* (think of the English word *epiphany*). It means "a visible manifestation," "an appearing." Jesus' return will be visible. It won't be a "spiritual" return that only a select few know about. When Jesus comes to earth in glory, the whole world will see him. Some examples of this word in the New Testament can be found in 1 Timothy 6:14 and 2 Timothy 4:8.

The Wonder of His Coming

When Jesus returns at the end of the tribulation to rescue his people and to destroy his enemies, his appearing will rock the universe. Most of the inhabitants of the earth will be shocked to see Jesus' arrival. The Antichrist will be on the verge of a great victory over the Jewish people and over the followers of Christ, and, suddenly, everything will be reversed. His armies will collapse on the spot. The Antichrist's empire will crumble. Every evil person will be found and judged.

The Antichrist himself will be taken and cast alive into a "fiery lake of burning sulfur" (Revelation 19:20 NIV). He will be joined by his helper, the False Prophet. Since the apostle Paul says in Philippians 2:10-11 that ultimately every tongue will confess that Jesus is Lord and every person's knee will bow in submission to Jesus, it's safe to assume that before these two instruments of satanic oppression are sent into eternity, they will bow to Christ and confess that Jesus is indeed Lord, even over them. One thousand years later when Satan is cast into that same fiery place, the Bible says that the Beast and the False Prophet are still there. There will be no escape.

While the unbelieving world will mourn and grieve over Jesus' return, the righteous will rejoice! The people of Israel who survive the Antichrist's onslaught will turn in faith to their true Messiah, the Lord Jesus Christ. The followers of Jesus who survive the tribulation will praise God that they have remained faithful through the darkest days of persecution and oppression. Believers on the earth will realize that the glorious days of the kingdom are about to begin. More than that, they will realize that they are about to hear commendation from the Lord himself— "Well done, good and faithful servant! Enter into the joy of my kingdom."

> I saw heaven opened, and behold, a white horse, and He who sat on it is called Faithful and True. . . . His name is called The Word of God.
>
> Revelation 19:11, 13 NASB

Something to Ponder

The rapture could happen at any moment. No prediction of Scripture has to be fulfilled before the rapture can occur. But the New Testament gives Christians plenty of "signs" to look for before the return of Jesus to earth in glory and power:

- Wars, famines, earthquakes, and other cosmic disturbances (Matthew 24:6-8, 29).

- Persecution of believers and hatred from the unbelieving world (Matthew 24:9-13, 21-22).

- Many "believers" will turn away from the faith (Matthew 24:10-13; 1 Timothy 4:1; 2 Timothy 3:1-5; 2 Peter 3:3-4).

- False Christs and false prophets who will deceive many with miracles and wonders (Matthew 24:11, 23-26).

- The "man of lawlessness" (the Antichrist) will be revealed (2 Thessalonians 2:1-12).

- And, in stunning contrast to the rest of the signs, the gospel message will be preached to all nations (Matthew 24:14).

Further Insight

In the past, it was popular to view the book of Revelation as the unfolding of world history between the first century and the present day. Many of those historicist interpreters thought that World War I was the battle of Armageddon predicted in Revelation 16. They pointed to the fact that the Turkish Empire (or, the Ottoman Empire) was defeated and that Jerusalem came under Western control. They fully expected the return of Christ to be the next event! Then World War II came around, an even more devastating war, and this view of Revelation began to fade.

Points to Remember

- At the end of the tribulation, the Antichrist and his armies will surround the city of Jerusalem and seek to destroy it—and they will almost succeed!

- Just at the moment everything seems lost, Jesus will arrive in splendor and majesty and destroy the enemies of his people.

Rapture or Return—Keeping Them Straight

Many Christians believe that the second coming of Christ will be a single event at the very end of human history. Jesus will return, the final judgment will begin, and believers will be ushered into their eternal home. Other Christians believe that the second coming will occur in two parts or two phases—Jesus will come *for* his church first in the rapture, and then later Jesus will come *with* his church in the return.

Prophecy students who see two phases in the second coming of Christ believe that the unfolding of the events of the end times has been progressive. In the Old Testament, where the emphasis was on Israel's kingdom, the return of Christ in power and majesty was the focus. Even in the Gospels, much of Jesus' teaching on the future focused on his final return. It was only in the New Testament letters, especially the writings of the apostle Paul, that the "mystery" of the rapture was revealed. One generation of believers in this age will not experience physical death. They will be caught up in the air to be with the Lord.

I saw someone like a son of man coming with the clouds of heaven. . . . He was given authority, honor, and sovereignty.

Daniel 7:13–14 NLT

They will see the Son of Man coming in a cloud with power and great glory.

Luke 21:27 HCSB

The following chart will help you compare the two phases of Jesus' second coming:

The Two Phases of Jesus' Second Coming

Rapture	Return
Jesus will come in the air.	Jesus will come to the earth.
Jesus will come to remove his followers from the earth.	The raptured church will come with Jesus in glory.
The rapture is not predicted in the Old Testament.	The return of Christ is often predicted in the Old Testament.
There are no "signs" of the rapture; it could happen at any moment.	There are many signs to look for.
Believers will be the only people directly affected.	The nation of Israel and the nations of the world will be directly affected by Jesus' return.
Only Christians will see Jesus.	The entire world will see Jesus.
The tribulation will begin (or continue) after the rapture.	The kingdom age will begin after Jesus' return.
Key New Testament passage: 1 Thessalonians 4:13–18	Key New Testament passage: Revelation 19:11–16

Digging Deeper

 You will sometimes hear the second coming of Christ called "the second advent." The word *advent* means "coming" or "arrival" and is usually used to refer to Christ's first coming to earth. The Christmas season is the season of Advent in the church calendar. The "second advent" anticipates Christ's return to earth a second time to raise the dead and to reward the faithful. Some churches or denominations will describe themselves as "Adventists" because they emphasize the Lord's soon return to earth.

Other End-Times Wars

Jesus warned that the entire tribulation period would be marked by war and the threat of war (Matthew 24:6). In the book of Revelation, one of the four horsemen that sweep across the world early in the tribulation is a rider on a red horse who takes peace from the earth and who leaves the devastation of war in his path (Revelation 6:4). Millions of people will die as regional wars lead to famine and disease (Revelation 6:8).

✷

The Bible also talks about other future wars—some on earth and some in heaven:

The Antichrist and the Enemy from the North

Time: middle of the tribulation   Place: the land of Israel

The prophet Ezekiel in chapters 38 and 39 of his book talked about a future invasion of the land of Israel by an enemy from the far north. The enemy is from the land of Magog, and their ruler is called Gog. The leader of this northern army is said to be the prince of Rosh, Meshech, and Tubal (Ezekiel 38:1-2 NASB). Prophecy buffs have tried for years to equate Rosh with Russia and Meshech with Moscow. The words don't match, but the geography does. The only foe far north of Israel capable of such a massive invasion is Russia. Moscow is straight north of Tel Aviv and Jerusalem.

The northern foes will have allies closer to Israel—Persia (modern

You will soon hear about wars and threats of wars, but don't be afraid. These things will have to happen first, but that isn't the end. Nations and kingdoms will go to war against each other. People will starve to death, and in some places there will be earthquakes. But this is just the beginning of troubles.

Matthew 24:6–8 CEV

Says the Lord GOD, "Behold, I am against you, O Gog. . . . You will fall on the mountains of Israel, you and all your troops."

Ezekiel 39:1, 4 NASB

Iran), Cush, and Put (countries south and west of Egypt, such as Sudan or Libya; Ezekiel 38:5-6). They will invade at a time when Israel seems to be at peace. This fits precisely with Israel's condition during the first half of the tribulation. Israel will feel secure because she will have a treaty in place with a powerful Western ruler, the Antichrist.

The prophet Daniel in his writings talked about the same conflict, but he made it clear that the Antichrist will get involved in this war as Israel's defender (Daniel 11:40-43). The northern enemy and her allies will march toward Israel, only to be met by a combination of the Antichrist's defensive army and the powerful judgment of God. God, for his own purposes, will actually help the Antichrist!

It's possible that during this war the Antichrist will suffer a fatal wound. Miraculously, he will survive and will rise up to defeat Gog and his allies. It will take Israel seven months to bury the dead and cleanse the land (Ezekiel 39:11-16). The vast expanse of Russia will be added to the Antichrist's empire.

War Between God's Angels and Satan

Time: middle of the tribulation   Place: God's heaven

Tribulation battles are not limited to the earth! In the middle of the tribulation, God's holy angels, led by a powerful angel named Michael, will fight against Satan and his angels. Some Christians believe that this battle took place long ago—before the creation of the world. Other Christians think that this is a summary of what took place in heaven when Jesus died on the cross and rose from the dead. But John places this event right at the midpoint of the seven-year tribulation.

Contrary to what many people believe, Satan does not live in hell. Satan hates hell! Satan dwells today in the realm of our earth, but he has access to heaven—and he spends a lot of time there! In the Old Testament book of Job, God called Satan in for regular reports (Job 1-2). John in Revelation said that Satan accuses Christians before God day and night (Revelation 12:10).

What will happen in this midtribulation battle is that Satan and his angels will be denied any further access to heaven and will be confined to the earth. When Satan sees that he has only a short time before God's judgment falls, he turns his rage against Israel and against those who have come to believe in Jesus during the tribulation. A remnant of Israel will be protected in the desert by God for the final years of the tribulation, but most followers of Jesus will be hunted down by the forces of the Antichrist. (The whole story of this heavenly battle and its aftermath can be read in Revelation 12:1-17.)

> War broke out in Heaven. Michael and his Angels fought the Dragon. The Dragon and his Angels fought back, but were no match for Michael.
>
> Revelation 12:7–8 MSG

Further Insight

God has created millions of angels to carry out his will, but only two of them are named in the Bible. Gabriel (whose name means "Mighty One of God") is God's primary messenger angel. He is the one who brings important information to key players in the biblical drama. Michael (whose name means "Who Is  Like God?") is the leader of God's heavenly army and is usually portrayed as the defender of God's people. Michael is called a prince of angels in Daniel 10:13 and the archangel in Jude 9.

Myth Buster

Interpreters of biblical prophecy have tried to identify the people of Magog and the leader named Gog for two thousand years. They have been connected to the Goths (in the fourth century), the Arabs (in the seventh century), and the Mongols (in the thirteenth century). In ancient literature the land of Magog seems to have referred to the people in Anatolia or modern Turkey. In the last one hundred years, many prophecy students have seen the threat from the North as a reference to Russia, although that identification is not clear from Scripture.

Points to Remember

- Wars and threats of wars will characterize the entire tribulation period.

- In the middle of the tribulation, Israel will be invaded and will call on the Antichrist for assistance.

- There will also be war in the heavens as Satan is denied any further access and is confined to the earth.

- When Satan sees that he has only a short time before God's judgment falls, he will turn his rage against Israel and against those who have come to believe in Jesus during the tribulation.

- Gabriel is God's primary messenger angel. His name means "Mighty One of God."

- Michael is the leader of God's heavenly army and is the defender of God's people. His name means "Who Is Like God?"

Is America in Biblical Prophecy?

The United States of America is never mentioned by name in the Bible. In fact, no modern nation (with the exception of Israel) is named in Scripture. Some students of prophecy, however, believe that the Bible indirectly identifies the United States in at least three prophetic passages. Their conviction that these references are to be understood as the United States stems from their belief that the end times are near and the prominent place America holds in the modern global scene.

The first passage identified with America is Ezekiel 38:13, in which the merchants of Tarshish ask an invading army if they have come only to plunder and loot. Tarshish was the farthest western point in the ancient world (modern Spain today). Some interpreters see this as a veiled reference to nations to the far west of Israel, including the United States.

A second passage is found in Revelation 12:14. When the Antichrist takes control of the temple in Jerusalem, people from Israel (pictured as a woman in the passage) will flee into the desert. The apostle John

> Thus says the Lord God, "Are you the one of whom I spoke in former days?"
>
> Ezekiel 38:17 NASB

said that the woman was given "the two wings of a great eagle" (NIV). It is likely that his reference to the wings of an eagle is a picture of the swiftness and silence of their escape into the desert.

The third passage is Revelation 17–18, where the destruction of a great commercial center is described. Some interpreters believe the future "Babylon" will be New York City.

None of these passages refer directly to America. The best understanding seems to be that the United States will be part of the Antichrist's alliance and that America will be under his control.

What Others Say

Many [people] wonder if biblical prophecy refers to the United States in any way. The answer to that question is "no."

J. Daniel Hays, J. Scott Duvall, C. Marvin Pate

The two wings probably do not refer to modern airplanes but rather to God's delivering power.

John Walvoord

Further Insight

While the United States is not directly mentioned in Scripture, many Christians point out that the nation of Israel *does* play a significant role in end-times prophecy. Those Christians, therefore, are strongly supportive of the right of Israel to exist as a nation, and they want the political leaders of the United States to support and defend Israel against any attack.

Myth Buster

Popular prophecy writers and speakers are more likely to see the United Nations in end-times events than they are to see the United States. Ever since its inception, the UN has been targeted as the vehicle the Antichrist will use to achieve world domination. Every few years a prophecy teacher of some variety will come forward with a supposed plan hatched by the UN to divide the world into ten administrative districts (the ten-horned Beast) or to move its world headquarters to Rome or even to Iraq, to the ancient city of Babylon.

What Happens After Armageddon?

Many students of Bible prophecy believe that a period of seventy-five days will elapse between Jesus' return in power to defeat the armies of the Antichrist and the official beginning of Jesus' thousand-year kingdom on earth. They base this conviction on the last verse of the book of Daniel in the Old Testament. Daniel predicted that three and a half years (1,260 days) of intense persecution will come on the people of Israel. Then Daniel pronounced a blessing on those who are still on earth seventy-five days later.

There are several events detailed in Scripture that seem to take place between the visible return of Jesus and the establishment of his kingdom on earth.

• The remnants of the Antichrist's government will be removed from the earth.

> When the Son of Man comes in His glory . . . then He will sit on the throne of His glory. All the nations will be gathered before Him.
>
> Matthew 25:31–32 HCSB

• The Jews who survive the seven-year tribulation period will be gathered in the land of Israel and will be judged by the Lord. Those who have believed in Jesus as Messiah will enter the kingdom and enjoy its blessings (Ezekiel 20:34-38; 36:24-28; Amos 9:14-15).

> Many of those who sleep in the dust of the earth shall awake, some to everlasting life, some to shame and everlasting contempt.
>
> Daniel 12:2 NKJV

• The Gentiles (non-Jews) who survive the tribulation will also be judged. God will send his angels throughout the earth to remove all unbelievers. Gentiles who have believed in Jesus will enter the kingdom (Matthew 13:47-50; 25:31-46;).

- The bodies of those who believed in the true God during the Old Testament era will be resurrected. Their spirits (which have been in heaven) will be reunited with new, glorified bodies (Isaiah 26:19; Daniel 12:2).

- Followers of Jesus who died during the tribulation will also be resurrected (Revelation 20:4–6).

The key point to keep in mind about Armageddon is that it is *God's* war. He is the one in control. He will move the plans and ambitions of future world leaders to bring them together at the right place and time. Human beings on their own will not bring history to end. The end will come in God's time.

Digging Deeper

God enabled the prophet Ezekiel to see far into the future of the people of Israel. He promised that, after God gathered Israel from every place on earth, they would face a very personal judgment. Just as a shepherd uses a shepherd's staff to count his sheep, the Lord will require each individual Jewish person to pass under the rod of God's evaluation. He will separate the godly from the wicked, the believing from the unbelieving. The believing Israelites will be welcomed into Christ's kingdom; the unbelieving will be denied admission.

Something to Ponder

Great battles have echoed throughout history for hundreds of years—Bunker Hill, the Alamo, Gettysburg, Little Big Horn, Iwo Jima, Operation Desert Storm—but these battles will sink into oblivion when Armageddon comes. The greatest armies ever assembled will be crushed by one word, one breath, from Jesus Christ.

Kingdom Come: The Millennium

Jesus will return and reign over a kingdom of peace and rest forever—and faithful Christians will reign with him!

Contents

The earth will be filled with the knowledge of the glory of the Lᴏʀᴅ, as the waters cover the sea.

Habakkuk 2:14 ɴᴋᴊᴠ

Jesus Returns—and Rules!

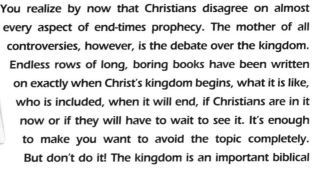

You realize by now that Christians disagree on almost every aspect of end-times prophecy. The mother of all controversies, however, is the debate over the kingdom. Endless rows of long, boring books have been written on exactly when Christ's kingdom begins, what it is like, who is included, when it will end, if Christians are in it now or if they will have to wait to see it. It's enough to make you want to avoid the topic completely. But don't do it! The kingdom is an important biblical promise, and every Christian needs to work at understanding it.

On two points all Christians agree! First, Christians believe that *Jesus Christ will return* to this world as the Judge of all humanity. He will return visibly and physically in majesty and power.

The second point Christians hold in common is that *Jesus Christ is the King*. Again and again the Bible declares that the Lord reigns as King forever. God the Father has placed all authority in his Son, Jesus. So—to be accurate—God the *Son*, Jesus, reigns as God's anointed King. He has always been the King, and he will always remain the King.

> The LORD is the true God; He is the living God and eternal King.
>
> Jeremiah 10:10 HCSB
>
> [God placed Jesus] far above all principality and power and might and dominion, and every name that is named.
>
> Ephesians 1:21 NKJV

And he rules over a kingdom even now. Everything that exists falls under Jesus' authority. His kingdom is everlasting and endures through all generations (Psalm 145:13).

So—if Jesus reigns and if he already reigns over a kingdom—why is there such a big debate over the kingdom of God? The debate arises from passages of Scripture that picture the kingdom of God as the visible reign of Jesus on earth. Revelation 20:1–6 (the key passage in these debates) says that Christ will reign on earth for a thousand years (a millennium of time). A lot of questions emerge from that passage: When will that happen? Is the kingdom coming in the future—or can it be seen today if a person looks in the right places? That is the heart of the debate—what does the promised kingdom of God look like and when will it come?

Something to Ponder

You may not be convinced that Jesus is King over all when you read the headlines or listen to the news reports of violence and war. That's why a person needs to pay attention to more than just the daily news. God does reign, but he is allowing an evil world to run its course. Even in the face of human rebellion against God's truth, God is in control. He is working all things together to accomplish exactly what he desires.

Digging Deeper

Christians have given three basic answers to questions about the kingdom of God. The advocates of each position believe that the Bible promises a kingdom. The division comes with respect to *when the kingdom comes* and *what the kingdom looks like*. All of the views on the kingdom are "millennial" views—that is, they focus on the promised one-thousand-year  (= a millennium) reign of Jesus. Each of these views is held by committed Christians who love Jesus and who believe they are interpreting the Scriptures correctly. What is needed in this debate are mutual respect and a dose of humility.

The Amillennial View—
The Kingdom Is Here Today!

Christians who hold this view of the kingdom of God call themselves *amillennialists.* Putting the letter *a* in front of the word *millennium* makes it mean "no millennium." Simply stated, they believe that there will be no *future* thousand-year reign of Christ on earth. Instead, Christ reigns right now in heaven and in his church on earth. Christians are in Christ's kingdom today.

The amillennial view of the kingdom is held by the Roman Catholic Church, Eastern Orthodox churches, and many Protestants. The foundations of this view are usually traced back to Saint Augustine, a fifth-century church leader and teacher.

In the Spotlight: Presenting the Amillennial Position

Amillennialists base their position on the following arguments:

• Jesus could return at any time. When he returns, Jesus will bring human history to an end in one big bang. Jesus will return to earth, all human beings who have ever lived will be resurrected (their bodies raised back to life), every person will be judged by God, and each will be sent to his or her eternal destiny. There will be no thousand-year kingdom on earth.

What I am saying, dear brothers and sisters, is that flesh and blood cannot inherit the Kingdom of God.

1 Corinthians 15:50 NLT

[The Father] rescued us from the domain of darkness, and transferred us to the kingdom of His beloved Son.

Colossians 1:13 NASB

• The "one thousand years" of Christ's reign mentioned in Revelation 20 is to be understood as a symbolic number, not a literal one. Nowhere else in the Bible is one thousand years mentioned as the length of the kingdom. John was using a large, round number to convey the idea of "a long time" to his readers. He did not expect them to take it literally.

- God did make promises to Israel in the Old Testament about an earthly kingdom of peace and prosperity. When Israel rejected Jesus as their Messiah, however, God transferred those promises to the Christian community—the church, the *new* Israel. All God's promises are being fulfilled spiritually today. Christians enjoy the spiritual blessings of God's kingdom now and will see the literal fulfillment of the Bible's promises in God's *eternal* kingdom on a new earth.

- Satan has been "bound" in this age, just as Revelation 20:1-3 predicted. This doesn't mean that Satan is inactive. He still opposes the work of God, but he can no longer deceive the nations.

- Jesus made it clear that the kingdom of God was "near" (Matthew 4:17 NIV). Was Jesus mistaken, or did the kingdom actually begin on the day of Pentecost when the Holy Spirit began to form the Christian community, the church?

- Those who expect a visible kingdom on earth have missed what Paul said in Romans 14:17, where he declared that the kingdom is not a matter of eating and drinking (literal activities), but a matter of righteousness and peace (spiritual qualities). Jesus reigns over his kingdom right now. He reigns in heaven over the spirits of Christians who have died, and he reigns on earth in his church and in the hearts of Christians.

Under the Searchlight: An Evaluation of Amillennialism

A lot of good things could be said about the amillennial position. Christians who hold this view have tried to deal with what the Bible says and, at the same time, keep things simple and straightforward. They have not become bogged down in endless controversies over minor details of prophecy.

Those who hold other views, however, have raised serious questions about the amillennial view. The main issues center on Revelation 20.

- Six times in Revelation 20:1–7 the phrase "one thousand years" can be found. How can you simply decide to call that a "symbolic" number that refers to "a long time"? It's true that the Bible doesn't refer anywhere else to Christ's kingdom as lasting a thousand years, but how many times does the Bible have to say it for it to be true?

> Assuredly, I say to you, there are some standing here who shall not taste death till they see the Son of Man coming in His kingdom.
>
> Matthew 16:28 NKJV

- John clearly placed the thousand-year reign of Christ *after* the return of Christ to earth in visible glory.

- Revelation 20:1–3 pictured Satan's "binding" as his removal from the earth to a place called the Abyss, a spiritual prison. This is certainly not Satan's condition in this present age.

- Certain aspects of the kingdom are functioning today. Christians know what it means to have Christ ruling as Lord in their hearts. But amillennialists look at only part of the biblical information about the kingdom. What about the promises to Israel of a glorious kingdom of peace and prosperity? What about the references in the New Testament to the *future* entrance of Christians into the kingdom? (Check out 2 Peter 1:10–11.)

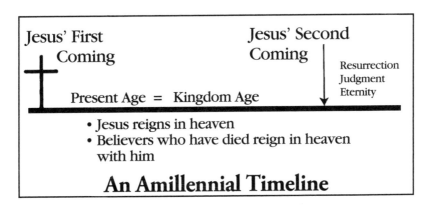

Jesus' First Coming

Jesus' Second Coming

Present Age = Kingdom Age

Resurrection
Judgment
Eternity

- Jesus reigns in heaven
- Believers who have died reign in heaven with him

An Amillennial Timeline

Further Insight

Many of Jesus' parables pictured the kingdom as the time *between* Jesus' first coming and his second coming, not as a time *after* his second coming. The kingdom is compared, for example, to a field where good grain and bad weeds grow up together until the final judgment at the end (Matthew 13:24-29, 36-43).

In the two thousand years since Jesus' first coming, the field of the world has been populated by both those who follow Jesus and those who don't. In a final act of judgment, Jesus will separate "the wheat" from "the weeds."

Something to Ponder

Plenty of verses in the New Testament say that God's kingdom is *now* and that Christians are in it right now. The apostle Paul said that when a person believes in Jesus, the person is brought directly into the kingdom of Christ (Colossians 1:13). So Christians are in the kingdom now. The only kingdom Paul looked for  beyond the present age was God's "heavenly kingdom" (2 Timothy 4:18). He doesn't say anything about anticipating a future earthly kingdom.

The Postmillennial View—
The Move Is Toward the Kingdom

A second view of God's kingdom is *postmillennialism*—the belief that Jesus will return to earth after a long golden age in which the Christian faith is embraced by virtually the entire world. Simply stated, postmillennialists believe that ultimately every nation and ethnic group will believe in Jesus as Savior and Lord and will seek to follow biblical principles. This universal embrace of Jesus will usher in an unprecedented age of prosperity and peace. At the end of that future age of peace, Jesus will return to earth and eternity will begin.

In the Spotlight: The Postmillennial Position

The case for the postmillennial view is based on the following arguments:

- The kingdom age will be brought about by forces already at work in the world. As more and more individuals believe in Christ, the social, moral, economic, political, and cultural life of the nations of the world will gradually be conformed to Christian principles until the entire world is "Christianized." This doesn't mean that every single person will become a Christian or that all evil will be gone from human society. It means that evil will be reduced to almost nothing.

> Turn to Me and be saved, all the ends of the earth. For I am God, and there is no other.
>
> Isaiah 45:22 HCSB

> This gospel of the kingdom will be preached in all the world as a witness to all the nations, and then the end will come.
>
> Matthew 24:14 NKJV

- The hope of a virtually universal salvation was anticipated even in the Old Testament. Isaiah, for example, called to the ends of the earth to be saved, and God promised that every knee would bow to him (Isaiah 45:22–23).

- Jesus did not picture the kingdom coming to earth suddenly. He pictured it growing, gradually increasing in size and influence. The kingdom will grow like a mustard seed until it fills the earth (Luke 13:18-19); it will work its way through society as yeast works its way through bread dough—silently and gradually (Luke 13:20-21).

- Postmillennialists base their view of the ultimate conversion of the world on Jesus' Great Commission in Matthew 28:19-20. Jesus' intention was that Christians would courageously do what he told them to do. The gospel message will succeed. Even the gates of hell will not be able to withstand the steady advance of the Christian faith (Matthew 16:18).

- The day is coming when the world's social, political, and economic structures will reflect Christ's lordship—and Christians should be working toward that goal. Once the millennial age comes, it will continue for at least one thousand years and will conclude with Jesus' visible return to earth, the resurrection and judgment of all human beings, and the ushering in of eternity.

Under the Searchlight: An Evaluation of Postmillennialism

Postmillennialists have made some very positive contributions to the Christian worldview. For one thing, postmillennialists have not been satisfied with a weak, stumbling presentation of the gospel message. They have pushed Christians to recognize that all of Jesus' authority stands behind that message.

Postmillennialists have also promoted an optimistic view of the future of human society. Some Christians who think that the world will get worse and worse tend to throw up their hands in despair and retreat into the safety of their church buildings. Postmillennialists push Christians to actively pursue justice and peace and racial equality and economic opportunity.

But is postmillennialism what the Bible teaches? Christians have raised some serious questions about it.

- No Christian questions the urgency of Jesus' final command to carry the gospel message to the ends of the earth. But while Jesus assured his followers of his authority and presence, he did not promise anything like universal reception of the gospel. The gate to life, Jesus said, was narrow—and only a few would find it (Matthew 7:14).

> How can I picture God's kingdom for you? . . . It's like a pine nut that a man plants in his front yard. It grows into a huge pine tree.
>
> Luke 13:18–19 MSG

- The present age is pictured in the New Testament as a time of persecution and difficulty for Christians. Sweeping revival has at times come to certain nations, and Christians enthusiastically pray for spiritual renewal today—but the Bible never promises a truly Christianized world.

- When the Bible pictures the kingdom growing gradually, it also pictures evil growing right with it. In Jesus' parable of the wheat and the weeds, the weeds (representing evil) were allowed to grow along with the good grain (representing the followers of Jesus). They were not separated out until the end of the age.

- Jesus himself wondered in Luke 18:8 if he would find faith on the earth when he returned. That suggests the number of genuine believers will be small when Jesus comes back—and yet postmillennialists say that Jesus will return to a virtually Christian world.

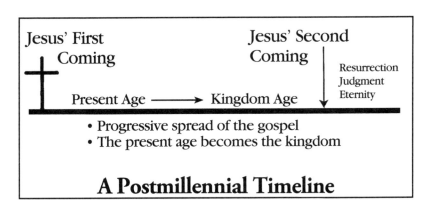

Jesus' First Coming

Jesus' Second Coming

Present Age ——→ Kingdom Age

Resurrection
Judgment
Eternity

- Progressive spread of the gospel
- The present age becomes the kingdom

A Postmillennial Timeline

Further Insight

Postmillennialists interpret biblical prophecy as nonliteral and spiritual. Their contention is that the Jews of Jesus' day were literalists who looked for an earthly, political Messiah, and as a result they missed what God was actually doing. Christians today who are literalists about end-times prophecy may miss what God is actually doing as they look for signs that the end of the age has come. Christians should be focused more on confidently declaring the gospel and advancing God's kingdom on earth.

Digging Deeper

The postmillennial position was widely held before the two world wars of the twentieth century. The Augsburg Confession (Lutheran) and the Westminster Confession (Reformed, Presbyterian) are basically postmillennial in outlook. In the twenty-first century, the Christian Reconstructionist movement has brought new interest in the postmillennial position. This group teaches that Christians should be aggressively pursuing the Christianization of political and social institutions in the United States. Several popular television personalities and Christian political commentators hold to a predominantly postmillennial view of future events.

The Premillennial View—
Jesus Will Bring the Kingdom

The premillennial view of the kingdom holds that Jesus will return visibly to earth *before* the kingdom age of peace. Premillennialists believe that the kingdom of God will be a literal, earthly kingdom of one thousand years during which Jesus will reign over the earth. The kingdom will arrive suddenly and powerfully when Jesus returns from heaven and defeats his enemies. Satan will be removed from the earth, and the effects of sin's curse will be lifted. Resurrected Christians and Old Testament believers will reign with Jesus over a renewed earth.

In the Spotlight: The Premillennial Position

The arguments premillennialists use to defend their position are:

- Premillennialism is the only view that takes Revelation 20:1–7 in its normal sense. Six times in this passage the Bible says that Christ will rule over a kingdom that lasts one thousand years. Also in Revelation, John makes it clear that the kingdom is established *after* Christ's return to earth in power and majesty (Revelation 19:11–21).

> The rest of the dead did not come to life until the thousand years were completed. This is the first resurrection.
>
> Revelation 20:5 NASB

- Premillennialists accept the fact that the kingdom is said to be one thousand years in length only in Revelation 20. But they add that the *concept* of a visible kingdom on this earth is taught throughout the Bible.

- Jesus came the first time proclaiming that the kingdom of God was near. He was not offering a kingdom *different* from the one God had promised in the Old Testament, but the *same* kingdom. He was not offering a purely spiritual kingdom (in the church), but a political and social kingdom based on allegiance to himself as King. Jesus offered himself to Israel as her promised King, but the people (as a whole) rejected Jesus and agreed to his death.

• God judged Israel for their rejection of Jesus in AD 70 when the Romans destroyed Jerusalem. Furthermore, God *postponed* the establishment of the visible kingdom until Jesus' second coming. Christians enjoy some aspects of the kingdom today, but the fullness of the kingdom will come only when Jesus the King returns to the earth.

• Most premillennialists distinguish between *Israel* (the people descended from Abraham through his son Isaac and his grandson Jacob; the Jews) and the *church* (all individuals who have received Jesus as Savior and Lord). The church is *not* the new Israel. Israel is still Israel, and the church is the church.

• The promises of an *earthly* kingdom cannot be generalized to refer to God's *eternal* kingdom. Kingdom promises are linked to specific places on this present earth.

Under the Searchlight: An Evaluation of Premillennialism

On the positive side, Christians who hold to the premillennial perspective have been far more serious about studying biblical prophecy than Christians who hold other views. Sometimes this interest becomes an obsession, but, all in all, premillennialists have tried to validate the Bible's strong emphasis on the future. Premillennialists have also tried to take the Bible's words seriously. Their concern for the literal interpretation of Scripture has motivated them to allow the Bible to speak for itself.

Christians holding other viewpoints aren't persuaded, however. They have looked closely at the premillennial position and have raised some interesting issues:

• Jesus spoke at length about future events on several occasions but never predicted a thousand-year reign. In fact, why is an earthly kingdom needed at all? Isn't it simpler to view Jesus' second coming as the climax of human history?

- God did make promises to Israel in the Old Testament about an earthly kingdom, but those promises were always conditional. God warned Israel again and again that her disobedience would cancel the promises of future blessing. The promises either have already been fulfilled (in Jesus' first coming, for example) or have been forfeited because of Israel's disobedience.

- Jesus said that the kingdom of God was "near" and "at hand." Was Jesus mistaken?

- When Jesus' disciples asked him about restoring the kingdom to Israel, Jesus did not say, "The kingdom is coming in the far future." Instead he told them that they would receive power to be his witnesses to the whole world (Acts 1:7–8). The church has obviously become the spiritual equivalent in the New Testament of Israel in the Old Testament.

What Others Say

A Premillennialist Speaks:

Premillennialism generally holds to a revival of the Jewish nation and their repossession of their ancient land when Christ returns.

John Walvoord

A Postmillennialist Speaks:

The millennium to which the postmillennialist looks forward is thus a golden age of spiritual prosperity during this present dispensation, that is the Church Age.

Loraine Boettner

An Amillennialist Speaks:

This millennial reign is not something to be looked for in the future; it is going on now, and will be until Christ returns.

Anthony Hoekema

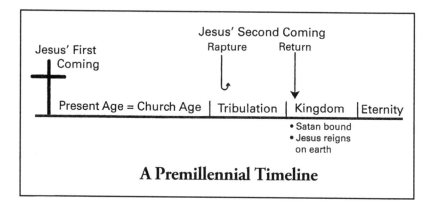

Jesus' Second Coming

Jesus' First Coming

Rapture   Return

Present Age = Church Age | Tribulation | Kingdom | Eternity

• Satan bound
• Jesus reigns
  on earth

A Premillennial Timeline

Further Insight

The view that Jesus will return to reign over a thousand-year kingdom was the view of the early church. Almost all the church leaders in the first three centuries after Jesus' resurrection held to a premillennial view. The fifth-century leader Augustine suggested that the kingdom of God was really a spiritual kingdom made visible in the earthly church (the amillennial view). Premillennialism made a comeback in the middle of the nineteenth century and is currently a very widely held view of end-times events.

Point to Remember

• Most premillennialists believe that the seven-year tribulation period will sweep over the earth just before Jesus' visible return. Human society will collapse under the weight of unrestrained evil and God's judgment. Premillennialists differ on whether Christians will go *through* the tribulation or will be raptured *out* of the tribulation.

Are You Convinced—or Confused?

While all Christians agree that Jesus is the King and that he will return to earth in glory some day, the three views of God's kingdom present three different pictures of what the future holds. The question most Christians ask (and it's a valid one) is: Which view is right?

But there's another question to ask: How should Christians live in the here and now in light of what they believe about the future? Each of the three views places responsibility on each Christian to live in the world in a new way.

If you hold to an amillennial view of the kingdom:

• *Live right now as a loyal subject of the King.* If Jesus reigns today as King, people around you should be able to see where your allegiance lies.

> This hope makes us keep ourselves holy, just as Christ is holy.
>
> 1 John 3:3 CEV

• *Stay alert for Jesus' coming.* Jesus told his followers that while he was away each person would be given an assigned task. But they were always to keep watch because no one knew the time of the master's return (Mark 13:32–37).

> We should be grateful that we were given a kingdom that cannot be shaken. And in this kingdom we please God by worshiping him and by showing him great honor and respect.
>
> Hebrews 12:28 CEV

If you hold to a postmillennial view of the kingdom:

• *Be courageous in your presentation of the gospel message.* Jesus promised that the gates of hell would not stand against the power of the church. Jesus calls Christians to meet a hostile world with absolute confidence in his truth.

- *Work to address the social and spiritual diseases of human culture.* The attacks against Christian morality are coming from all sides. Christians need to speak confidently, persuasively, lovingly, and passionately to a culture in desperate need of direction.

If you hold to a premillennial view of the kingdom:

- *Live as though Jesus could return at any moment.* Keep the approval of Christ in mind as you go through the activities of your day—places you go, words you use, attitudes you display, opportunities you encounter.

- *Purify your life.* The Bible challenges those who have the hope of Christ's return in them to purify their lives, to walk in holiness before the Lord (1 John 3:2-3).

Digging Deeper

The "kingdom of God" is a major theme in the New Testament Gospels. That expression occurs more than a hundred times in Mark, Luke, and Matthew (where "kingdom of heaven" is a synonym for "kingdom of God"). There are only three references to the "kingdom of God" in John's Gospel. One of them is found in a very personal encounter between Jesus and a man named Nicodemus. Jesus told Nicodemus that the only way to enter the kingdom of God was by being born again (John 3:3-5).

Points to Remember

- Jesus rules as God's King over all creation.

- Christians hold different views on what the kingdom of God is like and when the kingdom will come.

- Your view of the kingdom will have very practical effects on how you live each day.

What Dispensationalists Believe

Some premillennialists also call themselves "dispensation-alists," meaning they believe that God has dealt with his people in different ways throughout human history. The various eras of human history are called *dispensations*—thus the unusual name. Dispensationalism was made popular in the nineteenth and twentieth centuries by the study notes in the Scofield Reference Bible, a study Bible widely used among evangelical Christians. Many contemporary prophecy teachers and writers are dispensationalists and use that framework to understand the unfolding of biblical prophecy.

Dispensationalists see God using different "household rules" in different ages of history. Under the Law in the Old Testament, for example, God dealt with his people (Israel) in a certain way—animal sacrifices, worship at the tabernacle, lists of rules in the Law. Those rules changed when God moved to the present dispensation, the church age. The household rules will be altered again in the next dispensation, the kingdom age.

Dispensationalists do *not* believe that people have been saved in different ways through the ages. Human beings throughout all of history have been made right with God in only one way—by God's grace, through faith in God's promises.

We see that people are acceptable to God because they have faith, and not because they obey the Law.

Romans 3:28 CEV

You are able to understand my insight about the mystery of the Messiah. This was not made known to people in other generations as it is now revealed.

Ephesians 3:4–5 HCSB

The *content* of God's promises changes from one dispensation to the next. In the Old Testament, the believing Israelite expressed his faith by bringing the appropriate sacrifice that God required in the Law. In the

New Testament, the believer expresses his faith by following Jesus and living a Spirit-filled life. The content of God's promises has changed, but the *process* of salvation is always the same. Premillennialists who are not dispensationalists are called "historic premillennialists"—they believe in a future kingdom, but they do not think Israel will be the focus of God's program ever again.

Further Insights

Dispensationalists make a clear distinction between Israel (the literal descendants of Abraham, Isaac, and Jacob) and the church (those "spiritual" descendants of Abraham who have trusted in Jesus by faith). Other Christians say that the New Testament doesn't support that distinction. They believe that the division between believing Gentiles (non-Jews) and believing Jews has been broken down. The "new" Israel is the church, the body of Christ, and Christians inherit all the blessings that were promised to Israel in the Old Testament.

Something to Ponder

Some Christians find the study of biblical prophecy with all of its differing views a little too daunting. If you are a prophecy buff who enjoys reading and discussing the various views, have some compassion on those who don't get as excited about prophecy as you do. Let them get a word into the conversation too!

A Thousand Years of Peace

Most of what the Bible teaches about the blessings of Christ's kingdom is found in the promises God made to Israel in the Old Testament. Almost every prophet spoke to Israel of a future day of peace and rest on a renewed earth. Premillennialists believe those words apply to a future, earthly kingdom. Postmillennialists believe the golden age will come as the gospel spreads throughout the world. Amillennialists believe the promises apply to the eternal kingdom of heaven. Whenever God's kingdom comes in its fullness, the blessings will be magnificent!

A sample of the benefits that those who enter the kingdom will enjoy makes anyone wish for its soon coming:

- War will disappear. The Lord will reign as the Prince of Peace, and no nation will have need of anything. The industries that build the weapons of war will be focused on peaceful ends. In the words of the prophets, instruments of war will be made into tools for farming (Zechariah 9:10; Isaiah 2:4; 9:7).

> Just as water fills the sea, the land will be filled with people who know and honor the Lord.
>
> Isaiah 11:9 CEV
>
> He will offer peace to the nations, a peaceful rule worldwide, from the four winds to the seven seas.
>
> Zechariah 9:10 MSG

- Social justice, moral purity, and racial harmony will permeate the fabric of human culture. No more genocide or racial barriers or economic exploitation—just human society as God intended it to be (Psalm 72:1-4, 12-14; Isaiah 42:3).

- Physical deformity and disease will be eradicated. God the Healer will erase sickness and disability and deterioration (Isaiah 33:24; 35:5-6; 61:1-2).

- Long life will be the norm. Those who have children at a hundred years old will be considered blessed (Isaiah 65:20–22).

- The earth will be abundantly productive. Those who prepare a field for planting will work right behind those who harvest the crop (Psalm 72:16; Isaiah 35:1–2; Amos 9:13).

- Even wild animals will become nonthreatening (Isaiah 11:6–9; 65:25).

- The knowledge of the true God will extend to every person in every nation (Isaiah 66:23).

Sin's curse will be lifted in the kingdom. Joy and peace and contentment will fill human society. It sure makes you pray that God's kingdom will come.

Essential Old Testament Passages on the Kingdom

Isaiah 2:1–5	Isaiah 11:1–6	Isaiah 32:1–20
Isaiah 35:1–10	Isaiah 60:1–22	Jeremiah 31:1–40
Jeremiah 33:1–26	Ezekiel 34:22–31	Ezekiel 36:24–30
Ezekiel 37:20–28	Daniel 2:44	Daniel 7:13–14, 27
Amos 9:11–15	Zechariah 2:10–13	Zechariah 6:11–13
Zechariah 12:6–10	Zechariah 14:6–2	

Something to Ponder

There will be a lot of things missing in the kingdom that are part of life's scenery today:

- No hospitals, emergency clinics, or trauma centers—but birthing centers and (when a person is *really* old) assisted-living facilities.

- Pharmacies and rehabilitation centers won't be needed.

- Courthouses, jails, and police stations will crumble to dust.

- The Pentagon and military bases will be transformed into community centers and family garden plots.

A New Temple for a New Age

The last nine chapters of the Old Testament prophecy of Ezekiel describe a magnificent worship center in a restored city of Jerusalem. Some interpreters believe that this was Ezekiel's vision of what he hoped the temple would look like after the Jews returned from exile in Babylon. Others think that it is a vision of the heavenly temple. Many premillennial scholars believe that Ezekiel saw a millennial temple—a worship center that will be built in the future earthly kingdom as the center of the worldwide worship of Jesus the King.

Some parts of Ezekiel's vision of a restored temple fit beautifully with the idea of a kingdom temple. Solomon's temple (the first temple in Jerusalem) was beautiful but nothing like the grandeur of Ezekiel's temple. Even the magnificent temple finished under King Herod in New Testament times (the second temple) doesn't compare with the size and glory of the temple Ezekiel described.

He said to me, "Son of man, this is the place of My throne . . . where I will dwell among the sons of Israel forever."

Ezekiel 43:7 NASB

The problem with seeing Ezekiel's vision as a future temple is that animal sacrifices are clearly offered as part of the worship of God (Ezekiel 43:18-27; 45:17-23). Why would future generations in the kingdom offer animal sacrifices if the sacrifice of Jesus on the cross

The blood of Christ will purify our consciences from sinful deeds so that we can worship the living God.

Hebrews 9:14 NLT

eliminated the need for any further animal sacrifice? The Bible is also clear that the animal sacrifices of the Old Testament were only a temporary covering for sin, while the blood of the cross cleanses the believer forever (Hebrews 9:13-14; 10:11-12).

Those who believe Ezekiel's temple will be functioning during the future kingdom on earth teach that the animal sacrifices will not be offered to cover sin, as they were in the Old Testament. The millennial sacrifices will instead be a memorial to the ultimate sacrifice of Jesus on the cross. They will serve as a reminder of the price that was required to bring salvation to the human race.

Digging Deeper

In the centuries after the New Testament, Ezekiel's visions became the basis for the *merkabah,* or chariot, form of Jewish mysticism. According to this belief, by following various practices, the believer can ascend to a heavenly realm. By looking into his own heart, the follower will eventually be allowed to gaze at the heavenly chariot of God and the angels. The belief continues in the form of mysticism known as the Kabbalah.

Something to Ponder

When Isaac Watts wrote the song "Joy to the World!" he wasn't thinking about Christmas! He was writing about Jesus' second coming to reign as King over the earth. Think about the words: "Joy to the world! The Lord is come: Let earth receive her King. . . . He rules the world with truth and grace." This is a millennial carol! It celebrates the time when Jesus will reign over a world of peace.

Judgment Day— Our Accountability to God

Every person will someday give an account of their life to God. Some will receive his approval and blessing; others will find themselves separated from him.

Contents

Each person is destined to die
once and after that comes judgment.

Hebrews 9:27 NLT

The Judgment of the Cross

Some people do good things and never get recognized. Other people do bad things—horrific things—and never pay the price. It just isn't fair! Where's the justice?

*The Bible makes it clear that not every account is settled in this life. Every person faces a future evaluation—and no one will escape. The Judge in charge will know every fact fully and honestly. The law will be absolutely just and without appeal. Some people face this future evaluation with joy; many face it with dread. What makes the difference is **your relationship with the Judge**.*

One of God's major judgments is already finished. When Jesus died on the cross, Satan's doom and the condemnation of all who follow Satan in his rebellion against God were sealed. Satan used every deceptive tactic he could think of to get Jesus to avoid the cross, but nothing turned Jesus away from doing the Father's will. The death of Jesus as the full sacrifice for human sin sealed Satan's destiny in the lake of fire (Revelation 20:10).

If you belong to Christ Jesus, you won't be punished.

Romans 8:1 CEV

Now is the judgment of this world; now the ruler of this world will be cast out.

John 12:31 NKJV

The cross was also the judgment of God on all the sin of those who receive God's gift of forgiveness and grace. The judgment of God on human sin is that all are guilty before a holy God, and the punishment is eternal separation from the joy and presence of the Lord. But Jesus did something about humanity's desperate situation. He came and took the penalty that human sin required—and he offers grace to those who believe in him. Christians stand before God completely cleansed by the blood of Christ. No condemnation is waiting for those who have put their trust in Jesus.

Remember all this when Satan comes to you with one of his deceptive suggestions designed to turn you from the path of obedience and love for God. He is already a defeated enemy—and you are a forgiven child of God! The Holy Spirit living in you is far greater than Satan and all his forces (1 John 4:4).

Something to Ponder

 God the Father has given the responsibility of judging human beings to one person—to God the Son, Jesus Christ (John 5:22, 27, 30). The Father did that in order to be fair. Jesus has lived human life and been tempted in every area of life. Jesus can be a sympathetic, understanding judge because he has been here.

Digging Deeper

A few theologians have suggested that the time of Jesus' death on the cross was the tribulation predicted in Scripture. They draw parallels between Jesus' predictions concerning the time of the tribulation in Mark 13 and Jesus' arrest, suffering, and death in Mark 14–15. For example, darkness covers the land as Jesus hangs on the cross, and one of the signs of the tribulation will be the darkening of the sun.

The Judgment Seat of Christ

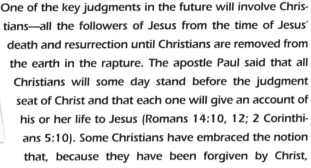

One of the key judgments in the future will involve Christians—all the followers of Jesus from the time of Jesus' death and resurrection until Christians are removed from the earth in the rapture. The apostle Paul said that all Christians will some day stand before the judgment seat of Christ and that each one will give an account of his or her life to Jesus (Romans 14:10, 12; 2 Corinthians 5:10). Some Christians have embraced the notion that, because they have been forgiven by Christ, nothing they do in life matters that much. Nothing could be farther from the truth.

Keep in Mind

As you think about the future judgment seat, keep several facts in mind. First, Jesus' evaluation on that day is *not* to determine whether you enter heaven or not. The issue of a Christian's eternal destiny rests on the fullness of Jesus' sacrifice and the person's faith in Jesus alone to save. No one enters heaven because of their good works or religious service; people enter heaven by God's grace alone. Second, Christians will not face punishment for their sins when they stand before Jesus. Those sins were judged fully on the cross and have been removed forever. The final fact to remember is that this evaluation will focus on what each Christian did in life with the gifts, resources, and opportunities that were given by God.

> We will all stand before the judgment seat of God. . . . So then each one of us will give an account of himself to God.
>
> Romans 14:10, 12 NASB

> The fire will test the quality of each man's work. If what he has built survives, he will receive his reward.
>
> 1 Corinthians 3:13–14 NIV

The outcome of this future evaluation will be either reward or loss of reward—or, to use a New Testament image, the "building" that each

Christian is constructing in this life will either burn up or bring honor from Jesus himself (1 Corinthians 3:10–15).

Whether you know it or not, whether you like it or not, you *are* building on God's construction project. The foundation of the building was

set when Jesus died on the cross, the blueprint has been approved by God himself, and each Christian is involved in building. What the Bible emphasizes is that each Christian has a choice of building materials. Christians can use eternal things to build with, or they can choose worthless things. The apostle Paul uses the elements of gold, silver, and costly stones to refer to Christ-honoring motives, personal integrity, and joyful obedience to God. He uses the elements of wood, hay, and straw to picture perishable things— sinful pursuits, selfish motives, pride-filled actions, and underhanded manipulation.

If you are seeking to serve God with commitment and in obedience, you are building with the right stuff. If you are coasting along with no desire for spiritual growth or no involvement in sacrificial ministry to others, you are building on God's house with the wrong stuff.

Tested by Fire

Each Christian's part in the building project will be examined by Jesus himself and tested by the fire of his heart-searching gaze. This fire will expose and destroy all the things that person has done out of selfish ambition and with wrong motive. Some of these things may look to all outward appearances like very noble and even sacrificial deeds, but Jesus will reveal the secret intentions behind them. On the other hand, the fire will expose other actions as true acts of humility and worth, even though they may appear at first to be insignificant. Each Christian will be rewarded on the basis of what remains. The gold, silver, and costly stones of obedience and faithfulness will be transformed into crowns of reward.

Running the Race

The whole picture of the judgment seat of Christ comes straight out of the athletic games of the New Testament world. After the races and games concluded, a dignitary— or even the emperor himself— took his seat on an elevated throne in the arena. One by one the winning athletes came up to the throne to receive a reward—usually a wreath of leaves, a victor's crown.

> Well done, my good and faithful servant. You have been faithful in handling this small amount, so now I will give you many more responsibilities. Let's celebrate together!
>
> Matthew 25:21 NLT

The Bible is not clear about *when* each believer will stand before Jesus. Some Christians think all believers will be evaluated just after the rapture. It's also possible that Christians who die before the rapture face the evaluation immediately after death. What is important to remember is that the judgment seat of Christ is not an encounter to be feared. You as a child of God will stand before the person who loves you with a boundless love, and his perfect love will drive out all fear (1 John 4:18). But the fact that you will give an account of your life to Christ should make you realize how serious the Lord is about how Christians live their lives as his children.

Digging Deeper

New Testament church-age believers aren't the only ones who will face an evaluation before Jesus. Old Testament believers were not looking for the rapture like Christians today. They looked for the coming of the Messiah's glorious kingdom on earth. Abraham and Job and Ruth will be resurrected after the tribulation ends and they will be ushered directly in the kingdom (Daniel 12:1–2). They will also face an evaluation in which their faithfulness to God will be rewarded.

Something to Ponder

The Bible says that some Christians will experience loss of reward at the judgment seat (1 Corinthians 3:14-15). Jesus will show that person what *could* have been his reward if he had only served him more faithfully, but all he will have to offer Jesus will be ashes, the burned-up remains of laziness, or the fruits of selfish motives. That man or woman will enter heaven—but be unrewarded.

Essential Reading on the Judgment Seat of Christ

Scripture	Summary Statement
1 Corinthians 3:1-15	A key New Testament passage on the Christian's rewards.
Matthew 20:1-16	Jesus' parable of workers in God's vineyard.
1 Corinthians 9:24-27	A passage on running the Christian life with integrity and endurance.
Matthew 25:14-30	The parable of the three servants; those who use wisely what the master has entrusted to them will hear his words of approval.
2 Timothy 4:7-8	Paul's confession of faithfulness in his life and ministry.
James 5:8-9	The Judge is standing at the door!

Crowns!

The word used in the Bible for a Christian's rewards is not the word for a king's crown but the word for the wreath given to the winner in an athletic contest. The rewards will be visible evidence of faithfulness to the Lord. But Christians won't wear those crowns for long! They will lay them before the Lord in recognition of his grace and his love and his mercy in salvation (Revelation 4:10).

✳

Crowns are rewards for those who remain faithful to the Lord and who work diligently for him. They are adornments that honor a Christian's labor for Christ in this life. Here are the different crowns mentioned in the New Testament:

- *Crown of life.* This reward is given to those who have endured faithfully through trial or difficulty (James 1:12; Revelation 2:10).

> Behold, I am coming quickly, and My reward is with Me, to give to every one according to his work.
>
> Revelation 22:12 NKJV

- *Crown of righteousness.* The reward given to those who eagerly look for Jesus' return and who live obedient lives in the light of his coming (2 Timothy 4:8).

> Now the prize awaits me—the crown of righteousness, which the Lord, the righteous Judge, will give me on the day of his return.
>
> 2 Timothy 4:8 NLT

- *Crown of glory.* A reward of faithfulness for those who are servant leaders in the church (1 Peter 5:4).

- *Imperishable crown.* A victor's crown given to Christians who run the race of life with integrity and discipline (1 Corinthians 9:24–27).

- *Crown of rejoicing.* The reward promised to those who are diligent in sharing the message of the gospel and bringing people to faith in Jesus Christ (1 Thessalonians 2:19).

The biblical promise of rewards is not meant to suggest that some Christians are more valuable than others. It suggests only that some have allowed the Spirit to work more deeply in their lives. Those who have been most faithful to the Lord on earth will likely be the last ones to focus on the rewards themselves. Their attention instead will be on the Giver of those rewards, Jesus himself.

Myth Buster

Some Christians are bothered by the idea of rewards or crowns for faithful obedience to Jesus Christ. They would say that they serve Christ out of love alone and not for any thought of reward. But the apostle Paul certainly wasn't ashamed to strive for rewards. He served Christ first and foremost out of love for Christ and out of gratitude for Christ's mercy, but he also had a burning passion to receive Christ's approval on his life.

Digging Deeper

In the Old Testament, the rewards of God were often physical or material blessings. In the New Testament, the idea of rewards shifts away from the immediate and earthly and focuses instead on the eternal and heavenly. Although there are places where Jesus speaks of rewards in this life (Mark 10:28-31; Luke 18:28-30), rewards are usually connected with the age to come. What is done during a Christian's time on earth will be rewarded in eternity.

The Antichrist Is Judged

God's judgment will fall on a rebellious world for the entire seven years of the tribulation. Sometimes several months will pass between judgments; at other times the judgments will come one right after another. It will not be an easy time for those on the earth. It's clear from the Bible that those on the earth will know that God is the source and cause of those future judgments, but judgment will not bring people to repentance. It will only harden their hearts against the Lord.

At the end of the tribulation, when Jesus returns from heaven in glory, several specific judgments will take place. The first person to be removed from the scene in judgment will be the Antichrist, the evil world ruler who has tried to set himself up as the object of the world's worship.

Toward the end of the tribulation, the Antichrist will gather a massive army in the land of Israel for a final assault on the followers of Jesus and on the Jewish people living in Jerusalem. For a while, it will seem certain that the Antichrist will crush all those who oppose him. But then the heavens will open, and Jesus will return to earth in victory and power.

The Master appears and —puff!—the Anarchist is out of there.

2 Thessalonians 2:8 MSG

The Lord knows how to rescue godly people from their sufferings and to punish evil people while they wait for the day of judgment.

2 Peter 2:9 CEV

The Antichrist and his sidekick, the False Prophet, will be condemned to the lake of burning sulfur (Revelation 19:19–20). The armies of the Antichrist will be destroyed by one word of power spoken by Jesus the Almighty King (Revelation 19:21). In one brief moment of time, the King of kings will take charge of his world.

As powerful in appearance as the Antichrist will seem to be during the tribulation, he's no match for Jesus. Jesus will overthrow him with the breath of his mouth and destroy his evil empire in the splendor of his arrival (2 Thessalonians 2:8). One puff of air from Jesus sends Satan's greatest instruments of influence away forever.

Digging Deeper

The beginning of the end for Satan will come in the middle of the tribulation when he is cast out of heaven and confined to earth (Revelation 12:7-9). During the earthly reign of Jesus, Satan is confined in a place called the Abyss but then is released for a short time at the end of the kingdom (Revelation 20:1-3). Finally the day will come when Satan and the angels who have followed him in rebellion against God will be condemned forever to the lake of burning sulfur (Revelation 20:10).

Something to Ponder

As amazing as it sounds, Christians will have some role to play in the judgment of evil angels. The apostle Paul said: "Do you not know that we will judge angels?" (1 Corinthians 6:3 NIV). Resurrected and glorified Christians will have enough wisdom and godly perspective to pass judgment even on angels.

Who Enters the Kingdom?

Millions of people will survive the tribulation period. Some of them will be loyal followers of the Antichrist; a few will be faithful followers of Jesus who have managed to escape the Antichrist's reign of terror. The Old Testament prophet Daniel implied that Jesus will take about two and a half months after his return to judge those still living on the earth and to sweep away all the remnants of the Antichrist's evil rule (Daniel 12:11–12).

✳

Four groups of people will enter into the earthly kingdom that Jesus will establish after his return in glory. Two groups will be in resurrected, glorified bodies; two groups will be in normal human bodies. All of them will dwell together during the thousand-year reign of Christ.

Redeemed Church-Age Believers

Christians who have been removed from earth in the rapture and who have received eternal new bodies in heaven will return from heaven with Jesus when he comes back to earth. As the apostle John saw Jesus' future return in the visions of the book of Revelation, he saw a vast army returning with Jesus. John described that multitude as the Lamb's bride who has made herself ready (Revelation 19:7). In other words, the bride of Christ, the redeemed church, will return with the Lord. Christians won't do any fighting as the Lord destroys the armies of the Antichrist. The only one pictured with a weapon is Jesus. The church will simply accompany their Lord as he reclaims the earth as his own possession.

I will bring you into the desert of the nations and there, face to face, I will execute judgment upon you.

Ezekiel 20:35 NIV

The righteous will shine like the sun in their Father's kingdom.

Matthew 13:43 HCSB

From every hint found in the Bible, redeemed Christians will live and reign with Jesus on the earth during the entire millennial kingdom. Those who have been faithful in this life in small things will be given greater responsibility in the kingdom. Those who have been faithful over a few things will be given responsibility over many things in Christ's kingdom. Christians will help govern the world ruled by Jesus the King.

Resurrected Tribulation and Old Testament Believers

The second group to inhabit the kingdom will be Old Testament believers and tribulation believers who are resurrected and given glorified bodies. John saw all those who had died in the tribulation for their testimony for Jesus raised back to life and reigning with Jesus for the thousand years of the kingdom (Revelation 20:4). These believers will be in eternal bodies but will have some part to play in the operation of Christ's kingdom.

Old Testament believers seem to be raised from the dead just before the kingdom begins. Their spirits are in heaven and will remain in heaven until Jesus' return to earth. Then the bodies of Abraham and David and Ezra will be raised from the dust and made new. Jesus said that Christians will sit down at a feast *in* the kingdom of God with Abraham and Isaac and Jacob (Matthew 8:11).

Surviving Jewish Believers

After Jesus returns and the armies of the Antichrist are swept away, every Jewish person in the world will be gathered into the desert of Israel. They will then be judged individually by the Messiah whom their ancestors had rejected and killed. Those Jews who believe in Jesus and receive him as their sovereign Lord will enter the thousand-year kingdom in their normal human bodies. They will live long lives and have extended families. Those Jewish people who have received the mark of the Beast during the tribulation and who refuse to believe in Jesus as the Messiah will be removed from the earth (Ezekiel 20:33-44; Malachi 4:1-3; Revelation 14:9-11).

Surviving Gentile Believers

The non-Jewish people (Gentiles) who survive the tribulation will also be judged by King Jesus. Some students of prophecy believe that the Gentiles will be gathered in the Valley of Jehoshaphat, east of the city of Jerusalem, for this judgment. Others think the Bible pictures the angels sweeping through the world and removing unbelieving Gentiles. Those men and women who have believed in Jesus and have been faithful to him throughout the tribulation will be ushered into Jesus' earthly kingdom and will enjoy its blessings for a thousand years. Those who have received the Antichrist's mark or who refuse to believe in Jesus will be removed (Joel 3:1-3; Matthew 25:31-46; Revelation 14:9-11).

> I will gather all the nations and take them to the Valley of Jehoshaphat. I will enter into judgment with them there.
>
> Joel 3:2 HCSB

Myth Buster

Some people don't like to believe that God will judge anyone. But judgment—the evaluation of what is good and evil or right and wrong—flows from the nature of God. Because God is holy and just, he must condemn evil. Because God is loving and gracious, he provides a way out from under his judgment through the cross of Jesus. Then God gives people the ability to choose to believe or to reject his grace.

Digging Deeper

Some Christians understand the final judgment of God as a series of judgments. Each is focused on a different group. Other Christians believe that all judgment will be delivered at one point in time. Different groups will be involved by one final judgment and will reveal the character of each human being to determine that person's eternal destiny. Some Bible passages seem to picture one final judgment event (John 5:28-29; Daniel 12:2). Other passages seem to point to different judgments at different times in God's program.

Something to Ponder

Judgment always involves a separation of the righteous from the unrighteous. Jesus used several judgment images in his teaching:

• Jesus gathers the wheat, but burns up the chaff (Luke 3:17).

• He welcomes the wise virgins, but denies entry to the foolish (Matthew 25:1-13).

• He separates the sheep and the goats (Matthew 25:31-46).

The Last Judgment

The final judgment of all time is the *great white throne judgment*—the awesome day when those who have rejected God's grace and love face separation from God forever. That day is not an easy one to describe or even to think about, but the Bible speaks about it in no uncertain terms. As difficult as it may be to envision people you know or love being sent into an eternity of separation and judgment, you can't escape the clear teaching of God's Word that such a day of reckoning will come.

One Final Rebellion

At the end of Jesus' reign on the earth, Satan will be released from his confinement in the Abyss (Revelation 20:7–8). During the one thousand years of the kingdom, millions of people will have been born, grown into maturity, and produced large, extended families to fill the earth. Many of these people will come to personal faith in the Lord Jesus; many will outwardly submit to Jesus' gracious authority but inwardly will not receive his grace and forgiveness and mercy. When Satan is released, those who have only outwardly conformed to the rules of the kingdom will be deceived and led into one final rebellion.

> I saw a great white throne and Him who sat on it. . . . And I saw the dead, small and great, standing before God.
>
> Revelation 20:11–12 NKJV
>
> I tell you the truth, those who listen to my message and believe in God who sent me have eternal life. They will never be condemned for their sins.
>
> John 5:24 NLT

A great host of people, like the sand on the seashore, will come against the people of God and the glorious city of Jerusalem. They will come prepared for battle and destruction, but there will be no war. Fire from heaven will fall and destroy them all (Revelation 20:9). Then Satan, that old deceiver and enemy, will be confined to the lake of burning sulfur where the Antichrist and the False Prophet were confined a thousand years earlier.

The Dead Are Raised

In John's vision of the final day of judgment, he saw a great white throne and the great Judge of all humankind seated on it (Revelation 20:11-12). At this point in God's plan—at the very end of the thousand-year reign of Christ on earth—all the believers throughout all of history will have already been raised from the dead and given glorified eternal bodies. The only people whose bodies will still be in the grave will be those who have not believed the message of God's grace. Unbelieving men and women from creation until the time of the final rebellion will be raised back to life. They will not be raised in new, eternal bodies, but in the same bodies they inhabited in life on earth. They will all stand before the Judge whose love and deliverance they had refused to accept. Those who chose to live without God in this life will find themselves separated from him forever.

The Books Are Opened

The people who will stand at the great white throne are not judged to see whether they will go to heaven or not. They made that decision when they chose to live their own way rather than God's way. They will be judged according to what they have done (Revelation 20:12). Unbelieving men and women will be judged to determine their degree of accountability and responsibility before God. One thing is certain—all the works that are recorded in God's books will confirm that they made the choice again and again to reject all that God offered to them and to go their own way.

The resurrection to condemnation and God's final judgment will conclude with an act of ultimate separation. Every unbeliever's knee will bow to Jesus Christ, and every individual will confess that Jesus is Lord.

Then every person who has rejected God's grace will be ushered away from the conscious presence of God forever.

> A time is coming when all who are in the graves will hear His voice and come out—those who have done good things, to the resurrection of life.
>
> John 5:28–29 HCSB

The Bible's account of that last judgment is presented in very sober terms so that each person who reads it will examine his or her own life carefully. God is not trying to scare you; he is trying to show you clearly what the future holds for the person who rejects Jesus and the grace God offers. The only way to escape the final separation from God is to run to the very person you have tried so hard to avoid—the Lord Jesus—and to fall before him in faith and trust and repentance. He will receive all who come to him.

Digging Deeper

The Book of Life is a record opened at the final judgment (Revelation 20:11-12). The book contains the names of those who have believed in Jesus as Savior and Lord. Every person who stands before God at that judgment will see with his or her own eyes that their name does not appear in God's book. Instead, these individuals will be judged according to other "books," which will demonstrate beyond any doubt that they have consistently rejected God's grace. No one will raise an argument against God's convincing justice.

Points to Remember

- Every person will some day stand before God for evaluation.

- Jesus, God the Son, will judge everyone with perfect justice.

- Those who refuse to accept God's gift of salvation in Jesus will face an eternity separated from the presence and care of God.

Check Your Understanding

- **At what judgment will Christians stand before Christ for evaluation?**

At the judgment seat of Christ, every Christian's works will be evaluated by Jesus. The purpose of the evaluation will be to determine the believer's reward or loss of reward from the Lord.

- **What is the great white throne judgment?**

The great white throne judgment is the final judgment of all human beings who have rejected God's grace and who have refused to believe in Jesus. Each person will be shown from God's record that they deliberately turned away from God's offer of salvation and forgiveness.

- **What determines if a person goes to heaven or not?**

A person does not enter heaven because of his or her good works. A person enters heaven because he or she has believed in Jesus alone and has received God's mercy and forgiveness.

Heaven and Hell

**The Bible takes a close look at your personal future too—
and reveals a lot about death and what comes after.**

Contents

I'm creating new heavens and a new earth.
All the earlier troubles, chaos, and pain
are things of the past, to be forgotten.

Isaiah 65:17 MSG

Why People Die

The Bible's picture of the future isn't just about wars and evil empires. There's also a very personal part. *You* have a future too—and that future extends far beyond your life here on earth.

The doorway to that future is an experience most people don't like to talk about—it's called *death*. Everyone knows that death is inevitable, but it's hard to think about or plan for or talk about to other people. What would help is *reliable* information about death and about what comes after death. That information is available in only one place—in God's Word, the Bible.

Condition

The word *death* is used in the Bible to describe three different conditions or experiences. The central idea in each case is separation. Death always involves separation.

- When the Bible talks about *spiritual death*, it means the separation of a person from a relationship with God. Spiritual death is the present condition of every person who has not believed in Jesus as Savior. Spiritually dead people need new life.

> The LORD brings death and makes alive; he brings down to the grave and raises up.
>
> 1 Samuel 2:6 NIV
>
> In [God] we live and move and exist.
>
> Acts 17:28 NASB

- *Physical death* in the Bible is the separation of the human spirit from the human body. At death, a person's nonphysical part (the spirit or the soul) leaves the physical body.

- The third condition called "death" in the Bible is the *second death*—the final separation of a person from God in eternity.

Cause

The Bible also provides some insight into why human beings die. If you look beyond the obituary, you will discover at least three causes for every human death:

- The most familiar factor is the *immediate cause* of death. This can be any number of things—a heart attack, cancer, drowning, a car accident.

- A second factor behind physical death is the *moral cause* of death. When Adam and Eve sinned against God, the entire human race was put under the shroud of death. Sickness, pain, suffering, and death are part of the human condition.

- Beyond the immediate and the moral causes of death stands the *ultimate cause*. The one who bears final responsibility for death is God (1 Samuel 2:6).

Digging Deeper

Jesus demonstrated his ultimate power over death during his earthly ministry by raising three different people:

- Jairus's daughter had died but was raised back to life by one command from Jesus (Luke 8:41-42, 49-56).

- In the town of Nain, Jesus raised an unnamed widow's son back to life (Luke 7:11-15).

- In his most dramatic act of power, Jesus called forth Lazarus, who had been in the tomb for four days (John 11:1-44).

Something to Ponder

Jesus came to repair what had been broken by sin. The first Adam lived in a perfect world created by God, but his disobedience cast a long shadow over the creation. Death came upon all human beings. The second Adam, Jesus, came to bring restoration and eventually an end to death forever.

What Happens After People Die?

What is it that will give you comfort when you stand at the grave of a loved one—or assurance when you face that last dark valley yourself? Most people want facts, not wishful thinking.

There is one person who has passed through death and come back to talk about it—and his word can be trusted completely! Jesus walked into the jaws of death, stripped it of its power, and conquered it forever through his resurrection. Then Jesus beamed a clear, bright light into the darkness beyond death's door.

Pictures

The Bible explains what death is like by painting some pictures—not with watercolors but with words. Each image is designed to bring comfort and peace as you think about death and beyond. If you are terrified by the thought of death, begin to replace those fearful images with God's pictures of what death will bring.

Everyone has to die once, then face the consequences.

Hebrews 9:27 MSG

I am convinced that neither death . . . will be able to separate us from the love of God, which is in Christ Jesus our Lord.

Romans 8:38–39 NASB

- The Bible most often pictures death as *sleep* (2 Chronicles 9:31; Psalm 13:3; John 11:11-13; 1 Corinthians 11:30; 15:51). Death, like sleep, is temporary and ends in a great awakening. The Bible uses the image of sleep so often because both sleep and death are universal experiences. From birth to old age, human beings need sleep. When a person is tired, he looks forward to lying down and letting sleep sweep over him. Most people don't fear sleep; they welcome it, and eagerly anticipate the arrival of a new day.

- Jesus described his death as an *exodus*, a joyful liberation (Luke 9:31). The dread of death keeps human beings in bondage and fear, but Jesus died to set his people free (Romans 5:14, 21; Hebrews 2:14-15). Death for the Christian is not a descent into darkness but a joy-filled release from the pain and disappointment of this life.

- Death is also like *taking down a tent*. These human bodies are temporary dwelling places—like tents on a camping trip (2 Corinthians 5:1). Human bodies are subject to disease and distress and despair. But Christians are confident that when this earthly tent is folded up in death, a permanent building from God is waiting in heaven. Death is the first step in the process that will bring a believer a permanent, changed-forever body that will never age or require a wheelchair.

- One of the most comforting pictures of death in the Bible is the portrayal of death as *coming home*. To most people, home represents a place of acceptance and rest and security. The apostle Paul describes two places the Christian can call home. First, human beings can be at home in the body, that is, in the present realm. To be at home in the body, however, means that Christians are away from the personal presence of the Lord. As much as Paul loved life and cared about the people he ministered to, he longed to be in the second place called home. Paul was confident that, when the spirit separates from the body in death, the Christian finds himself at home with the Lord (2 Corinthians 5:8).

- The apostle Paul also thought of death as a *departure* (Philippians 1:22-24; 2 Timothy 4:6). The Christian pulls up the anchor, unties the ropes that hold him to this life, and sails away. It's not a departure to an unknown destination. Christians depart to be with Christ.

Promises

As wonderful and assuring as the biblical images of death are, they are backed up by something even more secure—the solid promises of God. It's natural to look at death as an ominous foe, but God has given every

Christian a very specific promise that whatever death brings, it will not separate the Christian from God or God's love. The apostle Paul made a list of all the things that a person might think would separate him from God—and the very first thing on the list was death (Romans 8:38-39). God's promise to you in that passage is that not even death will be able to separate you from the Lord and his abundant love for you.

> We would rather be away from these earthly bodies, for then we will be at home with the Lord.
>
> 2 Corinthians 5:8 NLT

The Bible doesn't promise this kind of death to everyone. If you have never personally trusted Jesus, you *should* be terrified of death. The good news is that God offers you eternal life right now if you in faith receive Jesus. This life doesn't start after you die; you experience a whole new kind of life the moment you believe.

Something to Ponder

Elisabeth Elliot, a former missionary, tells about a time when she and her native guide were following a footpath through the South American jungle. The trail ended at a deep ravine. The only way across was a fallen tree. The guide jumped on and started across. Elisabeth stood frozen by fear. When her guide saw her hesitation, he came back, grasped her hand, and led her safely to the other side. At the deep ravine of death, every person hesitates. Then Jesus comes and takes his child by the hand and leads that child safely to the other side.

Digging Deeper

 Jesus made an interesting comment as he told the parable of the rich man and Lazarus (Luke 16:19-31). He said that, when the poor beggar Lazarus died, he was carried by the angels to paradise. That is the only reference to the activity of angels at the death of a child of God, but it opens up fascinating possibilities.

It may be that when a Christian dies, holy angels of God are responsible to accompany that person's spirit into the presence of the Lord in heaven.

Check Your Understanding

- **Why does the Bible compare death with sleep?**

Both death and sleep are universal experiences—and both are temporary experiences. Most people embrace sleep after a long day and look forward with anticipation to the new day. Those who fall asleep in Jesus look forward to their awakening in the dawn of heaven.

- **Where are the two places the Christian can be "at home" according to 2 Corinthians 5?**

Christians can be at home in their human bodies in this present earthly realm. The second option is to be absent or away from the body and to be at home with the Lord in heaven.

- **What is God's promise in Romans 8:38–39?**

The Bible says that nothing can separate the believer from the love of God in Christ Jesus—not the most powerful forces on earth, the strongest evil beings, or the most formidable foe, death itself.

Alternative Beliefs

Not everyone agrees on what happens after death. Just ask the people you work with what they think will happen after they die. If you ask ten friends, you'll end up with eleven opinions.

Most Christians believe that at death the human spirit separates from the body. The body is dead, but the spirit continues to exist in a conscious state. Those who have believed in Jesus and have been forgiven by his grace go into the presence of Christ—a place of comfort and rest.

People who reject the Bible's position that after death we continue to live a conscious existence in another place usually embrace one of the following alternatives.

Reincarnation

The belief that human beings are reborn to earthly existence after death is not new. The idea of reincarnation first appeared in early Hindu writings about 1000 BC. More than one-fourth of all Americans accept some form of reincarnation as possible.

Biblical Christianity has always rejected reincarnation. Human beings are not progressing upward to God through a long cycle of rebirths. The Bible says that men and women are lost and separated from God and are redeemed from that dreadful situation only by the grace and forgiveness of God.

You have decided the length of our lives. You know how many months we will live, and we are not given a minute longer.

Job 14:5 NLT

I want to die and be with Christ, because that would be much better.

Philippians 1:23 CEV

When Jesus was crucified, a thief on the cross next to his admitted his own sin and asked Jesus to remember him with favor in the future. Jesus did not promise the man a higher incarnation in the next life. Jesus instead told him that he would be with Jesus in paradise that very day (Luke 23:43).

Soul Sleep

Some religious groups teach that at death the soul sleeps, just like the body sleeps. Their argument is that a human being is a unit—body and soul (or spirit) functioning together to make a person. Therefore, when the body ceases to function, so does the soul. In this view, the body and the soul sleep until the resurrection, when the full person (body and soul) is awakened to face eternity.

The New Testament, however, makes it clear that the human spirit exists in a state of consciousness, apart from the body. In the apostle John's vision, he saw under the altar in heaven the *souls* of those who had been slain. These souls cried out to God, understood God's reply, and were consciously aware of events, both in heaven and on earth (Revelation 6:9-11). The souls were separate from their human bodies but were conscious and responsive.

Annihilation

Many people think that when a human being dies, that human being simply ceases to exist. Secularists believe that this life is all there is and that to embrace a belief in life after death is irrational. There simply is not proof (in their minds) that human beings continue to exist.

The Bible clearly contradicts that view. The Old Testament writers, Jesus, and the New Testament writers all affirm that the human spirit continues to live after death and that the human body will some day be revived and restored. Is that objective "proof" of life beyond the grave? No, it's not proof in a scientific sense, but then no scientist has the resources to check it out! Christians take the Bible's word for it—and anticipate the dawning of a new day after the darkness of death.

Suicide

Many people have advocated suicide or assisted suicide as a solution to the suffering of those who are terminally ill or who have crippling, painful diseases. Assisted suicide is portrayed as humane ("it ends human suffering") and as the supreme exercise of individual liberty ("he or she has a right to die"). From a biblical viewpoint, assisted suicide is indefensible because it is based on unbiblical foundations.

> Since we believe that Jesus died and rose again, in the same way God will bring with Him those who have fallen asleep through Jesus.
>
> 1 Thessalonians 4:14 HCSB

First, advocates claim that death ends human suffering. That is certainly true for a person who has believed in Christ, but a deliberately shortened life may prevent another person from coming to the point of faith in Christ. The second foundation on which assisted suicide rests is the claim that death and the circumstances of death are matters that human beings have the right and authority to choose for themselves. But the Bible consistently says that the opposite is true. Death and life are the sole prerogatives of God.

Digging Deeper

Seven suicides are recorded in the Bible, and they are all portrayed as tragic, desperate events. The most notorious biblical suicide was the one committed by Judas Iscariot after he had betrayed Jesus. Suicide is never explicitly condemned as a crime or a sin, but throughout the history of the church, suicide has never been regarded as an act that pleases God. The most direct biblical statement has been the sixth commandment: "You shall not murder" (Exodus 20:13 NIV; see also Matthew 19:18; Romans 13:9). Since suicide is self-murder, it clearly violates God's command.

Points to Remember

- Jesus has conquered death forever.

- For a Christian, death is joyful liberation into the presence of Christ.

- Suicide is never the right answer to pain and suffering. It only inflicts more pain on those who are left behind.

Something to Ponder

Death is not the end; it is simply the doorway to a whole new realm of existence. But the decisions that affect your eternal destiny are made in this life, not after death. So put "death" on your life calendar! It will come someday. Every day you are building the legacy you will leave behind. Your destiny after death depends on just one thing—your faith relationship with Jesus Christ here and now. Popular truth? No. Truth? Yes!

The Good News About Hell

It might surprise you to know that Jesus talked more about hell than he did about heaven. In fact, Jesus taught more about hell than anyone else in the Bible. Jesus was never afraid of or ashamed of the subject. He made it clear to people on several occasions that he believed in a place of judgment called *hell*. Jesus didn't try to frighten people; he tried to warn them—and he offered himself in order to give men and women an alternative to hell.

A Real Place

The Bible describes two distinct places as hell. Jesus talked about the torments of Hades (hay´-deez), the place where the spirits of unbelieving persons go at death (Luke 16:22-24). Hades is a temporary place. The final hell is called the lake of fire, a place of eternal separation from the conscious presence of God (Matthew 25:41; Revelation 20:14-15).

> They will throw them into the blazing furnace where there will be weeping and gnashing of teeth.
>
> Matthew 13:42 HCSB
>
> Now I am alive forevermore, and I have the keys to death and the world of the dead.
>
> Revelation 1:18 CEV

The Good News About a Bad Place

The good news about hell is that hell is avoidable. It's optional; you don't have to go there. The Bible declares that *all* human beings are sinners by nature and by choice and that all deserve the hell the Bible describes. God would be perfectly just if he removed every person from his presence forever. But in his grace and love, God has provided a way of escape.

God gave his Son, Jesus, to die on a cross in the place of guilty sinners. On that cross Jesus took the judgment that humanity deserved. But the cross wasn't the end of the story. Three days later Jesus burst out of the grave—alive. He broke the power of sin and death and hell forever. Jesus offers salvation freely to all who will believe in him. He gives the believer life, eternal life—not death, not hell, but heaven. If you have believed in Jesus as your Savior and Lord, you will never experience hell.

Something to Ponder

The Roman Catholic Church teaches that those who die at peace with the church but who are not yet perfect must undergo purifying suffering in a place called purgatory. Purgatory prepares the soul for heaven by purging out sinful or unholy traits. Belief in purgatory comes from the teaching authority of the Catholic Church and not directly from the Bible. Protestant Christians argue that no verse of Scripture supports a belief in purgatory, but rather Scripture seems to teach that the believer goes immediately into Christ's presence at death.

Digging Deeper

The Greek word *gehenna* (ge-hen´-a) is used twelve times in the New Testament to refer to the place of eternal separation from God. The original word referred to a valley outside the city walls of Jerusalem. The valley was used as a garbage dump, and fires burned continually there. The word came to be used as a cultural symbol of hell. (Jesus uses the word *gehenna* in Matthew 5:22, 29-30; 10:28; 18:9; 23:15, 33; it is usually translated *hell*.)

Heaven Today

If you have survived reading all the bad news about the future—wars, judgment, evil rulers—you are ready for some good news! God has prepared a wonderful place for his people, a place called "heaven."

Some people don't get very excited when they think about heaven. They view it as an eternal church service—or they picture themselves bored to tears as they sit around on a cloud strumming a harp. This popular picture of heaven is not the picture the Bible paints.

There are two paths a Christian may take to arrive in heaven. First path: Christians go to heaven when they die. The spirits of people who have received God's gift of salvation are taken "to heaven." Path two to get into heaven will be experienced by one generation of Christians only—the generation that will be taken to heaven when Jesus returns for his people in the rapture.

The heaven Christians think of today is also called (by Jesus) "my Father's house" (John 14:1-3). Jesus told his disciples that he was leaving them for a time, and while he was gone he would be preparing a place for them in his Father's

> I am going away to prepare a place for you. If I go away and prepare a place for you, I will come back and receive you to Myself.
>
> John 14:2–3 HCSB
>
> They marvel at how expectantly you await the arrival of [God's] Son.
>
> 1 Thessalonians 1:10 MSG

house. Jesus is preparing a place for his people—but he is also preparing his people for that place. Two building projects are going on! As you respond obediently and faithfully to the trials and challenges of this life, you are being gradually changed to be like Jesus. Heaven is a prepared place for prepared people.

So "Heaven—Phase One" is a beautiful place of rest and joy. It's the place where Jesus is right now. It's the place where the spirits of believers are taken at the time of death to be with Christ. But as wonderful as that place is, it's only temporary. An even better place is yet to come.

Myth Buster

 In the King James Version of the Bible, John 14:2 reads: "In my Father's house are many *mansions*" (emphasis added)—which has led some Christians to believe that personal palaces wait for them in heaven. *Heaven will* be a place of incredible beauty, but please don't envision rows of mansions. The word means "dwelling places." The focus of heaven will be on Jesus, not on the size of the house you live in.

Something to Ponder

Heaven is already teeming with activity! Two groups inhabit heaven today:

- Heaven is the dwelling place of God's angels (Matthew 18:10).

- The spirits of believers who have died are also in heaven.

- Those groups join Jesus, who ascended to heaven in his resurrected human body.

Heaven does not and cannot contain God the Father or the Holy Spirit. They are pure spirit and are infinitely greater than the creation.

The Future of Heaven

The Bible's promise of heaven includes a future phase as well. At the end of Jesus' kingdom on earth, after all judgments are over, this present earth and universe will vanish. Human sinfulness has corrupted every part of it. Jesus said that heaven and earth were in the process of passing away (Matthew 24:35) and some day will come to an end. When the old world is gone, God will step in and create a new place for his people.

In an amazing vision of God's future permanent home for his people, the apostle John saw four new things:

- First, he saw a *newly created heaven* (Revelation 21:1). This is not just a patched-up, reworked edition of the old universe, but something totally new.

> I saw a new heaven and a new earth, for the first heaven and the first earth had passed away, and the sea existed no longer.
>
> Revelation 21:1 HCSB
>
> God has promised us a new heaven and a new earth, where justice will rule. We are really looking forward to that!
>
> 2 Peter 3:13 CEV

- Second, John saw *a new earth* (Revelation 21:1). In some ways the new earth will be like the present earth—a world of beauty and order and wonder—but there will also be some differences. No oceans will separate the nations or peoples on the new earth. The new earth probably won't rotate because John said there is no night (Revelation 21:25).

- Third, John saw that *everything in the future creation will be new.* There will be new dictionaries in that new earth—filled with new words to describe its wonders.

- The fourth thing John saw was *a magnificent city* (Revelation 21:2–3). The final home for God's people for eternity will be a dazzling city, designed and built by God. It is a *holy* city too—uncorrupted by evil.

People will enter the city from all directions. They will come from every ethnic group, from every level of society, from every denominational tradition, and from every generation since the beginning of time. But they will all be bound together by faith in and devotion to Jesus Christ.

Something to Ponder

Some things from this earth will be missing in the new creation, but they won't be missed. Sin's curse will be gone forever, along with the disease, decay, and injustice that came with it. Death, sorrow, suffering, and pain won't be there either. John saw no hospitals or cemeteries or prisons! There won't even be any church buildings. The Lord God and Jesus the Lamb are the temple of worship.

Digging Deeper

The angel who gave John the guided tour of the new earth measured the future city. Its width, length, and height are equal, making a cube or pyramid fourteen hundred miles on each side. That is roughly the distance from the Mississippi River to the Atlantic Ocean and from the U.S.-Canadian border to the Gulf of Mexico. If that isn't massive enough, it stretches from the earth's surface one-twentieth of the way to the moon!

What People Will Do for Eternity

A new city on a new earth sounds like a spectacular place for the eternal home of God's people. If you think about eternity for very long, however, you might begin to wonder what you will do with all that time. What will fill the hours and days and years of eternity? Worshiping the Lord may be engaging for a year—or a hundred years—but eventually you will have to find new things to do.

Actually, heaven will be a place of complete fulfillment and limitless opportunities. At least five activities will fill every person's life in heaven.

Worship

Christians will spend time in joyful, spontaneous, genuine worship to God and to Jesus the Lamb. God's people will sing and praise God—and they won't be distracted by time or get tired physically. You will stand and kneel and fall on your face, and you won't really care what those around you think. All you will care about is that God knows how much you love him. If you are expecting quiet, solemn worship in heaven, clothed in hushed tones and accompanied by soft organ music, you will be disappointed. Heaven's worship will be punctuated by shouts, exuberant voices, trumpets, and spontaneous singing.

I heard all beings . . . saying, "Praise, honor, glory, and strength forever and ever to the one who sits on the throne and to the Lamb!"

Revelation 5:13 CEV

The throne of God and of the Lamb will be in [the city], and His bond-servants will serve Him.

Revelation 22:3 NASB

Ministry

Eight times in the book of Revelation the apostle John said that the people in heaven will serve God. Most readers wish John had been a little more specific about what that service will involve! How can you serve when people will have so few needs? As you think 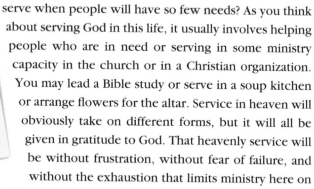 about serving God in this life, it usually involves helping people who are in need or serving in some ministry capacity in the church or in a Christian organization. You may lead a Bible study or serve in a soup kitchen or arrange flowers for the altar. Service in heaven will obviously take on different forms, but it will all be given in gratitude to God. That heavenly service will be without frustration, without fear of failure, and without the exhaustion that limits ministry here on earth. The work will be enriching, challenging, and fulfilling far beyond anything experienced in this life.

Fellowship

Every believer in heaven will enjoy the company of millions of other believers—and Jesus himself (Hebrews 12:22-24). Christians will relax around the table with Elijah and Abraham and Paul and Mary—and time will be abundant to ask every question you have ever wanted to ask. Instead of focusing on your own agenda, you will be able to focus all your attention and energy on others.

Learning

Christians won't know everything when they get to heaven—but they will have an infinite capacity to learn. They will learn about one another, they will explore God's newly created earth, and they will learn more and more about the depths of God's mercy. Think of all the things you have had an interest in doing but have never had the time or opportunity to pursue—playing the cello, rock climbing, learning to paint. Heaven will be a place of limitless opportunities.

Rest

Heaven will be a place of perfect wholeness. God's people will enjoy his rest. It won't be rest from work or weariness—resurrected bodies don't get tired! It will be rest from want, the empowering, energizing rest found in God's presence alone. In heaven God's people will be perfectly content and satisfied forever.

> God did this so that in the future world he could show how truly good and kind he is to us because of what Christ Jesus has done.
>
> Ephesians 2:7 CEV

Sounds like a place you want to go to, doesn't it? But God hasn't told Christians about heaven's glory so they will dress in white robes and sit on a mountaintop waiting for Jesus to come. He has told Christians what lies ahead so that they will live courageous, faithful lives here and now. The apostle Peter, as he contemplated the joy of heaven, challenged his readers with this question: "Since everything will be destroyed in this way, what kind of people ought you to be?" (2 Peter 3:11 NIV). His answer was to urge Christians to live holy and godly lives as they look forward to the return of Christ and the prospect of an eternity in heaven. How will you respond to God's challenge? Make every effort, the Bible says, to be found blameless and at peace with Christ.

Digging Deeper

The Bible uses the word *heaven* in three senses. The first heaven is the air, the atmosphere of the earth, in which birds fly. The second heaven is the cosmic heavens, the place of the planets and stars. The third heaven is the dwelling place of God and his angels. When the apostle Paul said that he was taken into the third heaven, he meant that he was transported into the heaven of God (2 Corinthians 12:2). The Holy Spirit was sent from heaven (1 Peter 1:12), and Jesus will return from heaven (Revelation 19:11–14).

Something to Ponder

Before Jesus' resurrection, the spirits of believers who died went to a place of rest and comfort called "Abraham's bosom" or "Abraham's side" (Luke 16:22). It was a temporary dwelling place for the redeemed until Jesus came, died on the cross, and rose again. When Jesus ascended back into heaven, it seems that he took the spirits of believers into God's heaven with him. Abraham and David and Ruth from the Old Testament are with Christ today but are still waiting for the resurrection of their bodies in the future.

Points to Remember

• Christians who die go to be with Jesus in the Father's house.

• The eternal home of God's people will be a magnificent city on a new earth.

• Heaven will be a place of limitless opportunity, spontaneous worship, and joy-filled fellowship.

Seven Questions About Heaven

Probably no biblical subject prompts more questions than the subject of heaven. What will heaven be like, who will be there, and what will people do for eternity? The Bible doesn't give all the answers, but some questions can be answered based on direct biblical information or at least on biblical principles. The fullness of heaven, of course, will be revealed only when believing men and women step from this life into the life beyond.

Seven frequently asked questions about heaven:

1. *Will people recognize one another in heaven?* It seems probable that they will! Jesus was recognized by his disciples after his resurrection.

2. *When people (or babies) die, do they become angels?* No! Human beings are human beings forever. Humans never become angels.

> We do know that [when Christ comes] we will be like him, for we will see him as he really is.
>
> 1 John 3:2 NLT

3. *What are resurrected bodies like?* People in heaven will have an eternal body, like Jesus' resurrection body. These present bodies decay and die; resurrection bodies will never die or deteriorate.

> Since we also have such a large cloud of witnesses surrounding us, let us . . . run with endurance the race that lies before us.
>
> Hebrews 12:1 HCSB

4. *Will people in heaven see God?* God the Father and God the Holy Spirit are pure spirit and have no physical form. Jesus is the only member of the Trinity with a human, visible form.

5. *Are there animals in heaven?* Since animals are such a wonderful part of this world, it doesn't seem out of character that animals would inhabit the new world as well.

6. *Will people experience the passage of time in heaven?* John says that the Tree of Life in heaven will bear a different fruit *every month* (Revelation 22:2). So people may experience time as we know it in this life, but they will never age or grow old.

7. *Do people in heaven today know what's happening on earth?* Some biblical statements imply that people in heaven do have knowledge of events on earth (Hebrews 12:1; 1 Corinthians 11:10; Revelation 6:9-11). They have God's perspective on events, but they seem to be aware of what God is doing on the earth.

Something to Ponder

In his vision, the apostle John saw some souls of people who had been slain (Revelation 6:9). These people were in heaven, but they remembered that they had been killed unjustly and that God was in the process of bringing judgment on the world for their deaths. This indicates that people in heaven are aware of what is going on in the earthly realm. Eventually God will wipe away every tear, but not until his plans are completed.

Myth Buster

Jesus said that people in heaven would not marry or be given in marriage (Luke 20:34-35). Some have concluded from that statement that people will be genderless in heaven. A better solution is that Jesus used a polite expression to mean that people in heaven will not reproduce and bear children. It doesn't mean that a husband won't remember that a particular woman was his wife on earth.

Practical Tactics for Surviving the Future

The big question that emerges from this look at biblical prophecy and the end times is this: What can Christians do today to get ready for God's tomorrow? Jesus said there would be two kinds of people on earth when he returned—the prepared and the unprepared. Which are you? It doesn't really make much difference what view you hold on the kingdom or the time of the rapture if you aren't prepared for Jesus' return. If he comes today, will you be ready?

✳

Here are some suggestions that will help keep eternity in the picture when you face the demands of another day.

Survival Tactic #1: Solidify Your Relationship with the Coming King

When Jesus comes, it will be too late! When you die, there is no second chance. The most critical decision you can make about the future is to believe in Jesus Christ as Savior and Lord. If you have never believed in Jesus, you aren't ready for the future.

Survival Tactic #2: Live as a Committed Follower of Jesus

Men and women are saved by God's grace alone—but once they come to faith, God calls them to a life of joyful obedience and sacrificial service to him. God not only calls; he also equips. God gives abundantly, and he expects his people to invest into his kingdom

We are His creation—created in Christ Jesus for good works, which God prepared ahead of time so that we should walk in them.

Ephesians 2:10 HCSB

Here we do not have a lasting city, but we are seeking the city which is to come.

Hebrews 13:14 NASB

what he gives them to use—natural abilities, spiritual gifts, resources of time and money. Christians have different levels of giftedness and varying amounts of resources, but what God looks for is *faithfulness* in using what he has given. Your faithfulness as a Christian today affects your future. You aren't just punching the clock or running a business to pay the rent and to buy a nice car. You are working to please your *real* boss, Jesus. If you want the future to be as challenging and fulfilling as it can be, faithfully serve God now in every arena of life.

Survival Tactic #3: Practice Your Praise!

When Jesus wanted to picture what the "forever home" of the Christian would be like, he didn't picture it as a church service or a theological

lecture or even a quiet but boring retirement home. Jesus pictured heaven as a party—a joy-filled, foot-stomping, hug-your-aunt-Mildred family reunion! Christians will sit down with Abraham and all the other well-known and lesser-known children of God for a wonderful, warm experience—and at the center of everything will be Jesus. The songs, the praise, the adoration will all be focused on him. Get some practice being joyful as a Christian! It will prepare your heart for a joy-filled eternity.

Survival Tactic #4: Keep Learning

Don't stop studying Bible prophecy just because you have come to the end of this book. Check out other resources. Keep reading the Bible with an interest in the predictions that have yet to be fulfilled. Don't just listen to the speakers and read the books that support the position you hold. Listen to what other Christians are saying, and measure everything (including your own position) against the Word of God.

Survival Tactic #5: Keep Looking for Jesus

Christians don't look for "signs" that the tribulation is approaching—although they certainly need to be aware of the events in the world.

Christians don't look for the Antichrist—although he may be on the world scene right now. *Christians look for Jesus to return.* Paying the mortgage, raising the kids, and pursuing a career are all important aspects of life—but they are not all there is to life. Overshadowing your steps, encouraging your heart, keeping you faithful when it would be easier to bail out is the rock-solid assurance you can have that Jesus is coming.

> The end of all things is at hand; therefore be serious and watchful in your prayers.
>
> 1 Peter 4:7 NKJV

Christians are sometimes accused of being so heavenly minded that they aren't much earthly good—but that isn't really the problem. The Bible challenges Christians to set their hearts and minds on things above, not on earthly things (Colossians 3:1-2). God has not told his people about the future so they will live irresponsible and lazy lives. He has told them about the future so they will live courageous and holy lives every day. Christians know how the story ends! Confidence in God and in his promises will give you the courage you need to walk through the fire of persecution—or to walk into your workplace tomorrow morning.

Digging Deeper

Jesus closes the book of Revelation by using a series of powerful titles for himself:

- "I am the Alpha and the Omega" (meaning it all starts and ends with him).
- "I am the First and the Last" (he's the final goal toward which history is moving).
- "I am the Beginning and the End" (the author and conclusion of it all).
- "I am the Root and Offspring of David" (he's the fulfillment of everything God promised to Israel).
- "I am the Bright Morning Star" (Jesus' return will signal the dawning of God's new day).

What Others Say

 The Christian life is meant to be like heaven on earth. Believers regularly taste the sweetness of the same heaven to which someday we will go to dwell forever. Praising and loving God with all your being, adoring and obeying Christ, pursuing holiness, cherishing fellowship with other saints—those are the elements of heavenly life we can begin to taste in this world. Those same pursuits and privileges will occupy us forever, but we can begin to practice them even now.

John MacArthur

Something to Ponder

The final prayer of the Bible is a sigh—a deep longing in every believer's spirit: "Amen. Come, Lord Jesus." Come, and take your people out of this world of sorrow and suffering. Come, and establish your kingdom of peace. Come, Lord Jesus. Please, come.

Blessed are those who are invited to
the wedding supper of the Lamb!

Revelation 19:9 NIV

All the believers, from righteous Abel down through the very last of the saints of God in the tribulation period, will share in the triumph of the Son of God. His is the victory, won at Calvary, but he shares it with all of his redeemed ones.

Donald Barnhouse

The sun will no more be your light by day, nor will the brightness of the moon shine on you, for the LORD will be your everlasting light.

Isaiah 60:19 NIV

The future starts now! God is keeping careful watch
over us and the future. The Day is coming when
you'll have it all—life healed and whole.

1 Peter 1:4–5 MSG

Books in The Indispensable Guide to Practically Everything
series include:

The Indispensable Guide to Practically Everything:
The Bible

The Indispensable Guide to Practically Everything:
Bible Prophecy and End Times

The Indispensable Guide to Practically Everything:
Life After Death & Heaven and Hell

The Indispensable Guide to Practically Everything:
World Religions and What People Believe